CATHOLIC PRAYER BOOK

WRITTEN AND COMPILED BY

FATHER ROBERT J. FOX

OUR SUNDAY VISITOR, INC.
Publishers
HUNTINGTON

This book

is humbly dedicated

to Our Lady of Guadalupe,

whose miraculous portrait

is reproduced on its cover.

© copyright Robert J. Fox 1972, 1974
All rights reserved.
ISBN 0-87973-771-9
Library of Congress Catalog Card Number 74-75133

COVER DESIGN BY JAMES E. McILRATH

Our Sunday Visitor, Inc.
200 Noll Plaza, Huntington, Indiana 46750

Nihil obstat: Rev. Lawrence Gollner, Censor librorum
Imprimatur: ✠ Leo A. Pursley,
       Bishop of Fort Wayne-South Bend
       December 10, 1973

20 19 18 17 16 15 14 13

Preface

One of the most encouraging and refreshing signs of the times has been the revival of books and aids for private prayer. An exaggerated emphasis on the place of community prayer, perhaps by reason of long neglect, has led to the virtual annihilation of the lonely, prayerful Christian who prefers the counsel of Christ that we sometimes, at least, withdraw apart for private personal prayer despite the broadsides of the innumerable liturgical commissions that we give up ourselves entirely to the community song festival and the collective bombardment of heaven (or one another) by the people of God in community. It is not always possible to invite the entire neighborhood, a segment of the people of God, into one's closet when one is disposed to pray in private, a practice which has the endorsement of impeccable, even divine, authority.

And so, while eagerly welcoming the joy and strength that comes from prayer in community, especially liturgical prayer, one is grateful for assistance in private prayer such as that which Father Robert Fox provides in his new and welcomed prayer book designed to meet the needs of contemporary Catholics. His manual brings together familiar prayers and devotions, together with new prayers appropriate for us all and appropriately adapted to special needs and vocations.

It is a pleasure, and a pastoral duty, to commend his book to the widest possible public. Prayer is to the life of the soul what breathing is to the life of the body; once it ceases, something dies. In the case of the soul, the thing that dies is the life of grace.

Father Fox has done his work with faith, fervor and pastoral zeal. May the prayers of those who use his book always include him — and the undersigned.

✠ JOHN CARDINAL WRIGHT
Vatican City
Easter, 1972

Introduction

This prayer book was designed to meet the needs of many a modern-day Catholic. Many have asked for a small and practical prayer book which would meet the daily needs of the average Catholic. Hopefully, this prayer book is the answer. It does not contain prayers for every possible circumstance, but it does contain prayers most frequently used.

Our Catholic Church buildings today, for the most part, are provided with aids to assist in the official liturgy of the Mass. Therefore, we have omitted the eucharistic prayers. However, there are valuable prayers which can be said before Mass. It is well to arrive in sufficient time to make a prayerful preparation. Other prayers are suggested for after holy communion and again for those who spend some minutes after the people are officially dismissed from holy Mass.

Especially helpful should be the aids provided for an examination of conscience before confession. A special examination is provided for young people. The examination is designed to remove us from routine confessions and to help us grow in self-knowledge and union with God.

Some contemporary prayers are found in this prayer book to meet modern needs. I have composed the prayers mindful of challenges in the modern Church. Also, I have desired to preserve the authentic Catholic faith of the past two thousand years. Our manner of prayer is indicative of our faith and our love. These prayers may serve to initiate the user into other individualized prayers which will keep him in daily union with God and better disposed for the great action of the Christian community, the sacrifice of the Mass.

FATHER ROBERT J. FOX
St. Bernard's Church
Redfield, South Dakota

Contents

A
CATHOLIC
PRAYER
BOOK

Clause Method of Praying the Rosary

(Recommended by Pope Paul VI, paragraph 46 in his Apostolic Exhortation, Marialis Cultus, Feb. 2, 1974. One adds to the name of Jesus in each Hail Mary a reference to the mystery being contemplated. This "clause" method has been mandated by the bishops of some countries, e.g. Switzerland, Germany, Austria, Hungary, etc.)

I. "Clauses" for the Joyful Mysteries:
1. ...Jesus, whom thou has conceived.
2. ...Jesus, whom thou has brought to St. Elizabeth.
3. ...Jesus, who was born in Bethlehem
4. ...Jesus, whom thou has offered in the temple.
5. ...Jesus, whom thou has found in the temple.

II. "Clauses" for the Sorrowful Mysteries.
1. ...Jesus, who for us sweat blood.
2. ...Jesus, who for us was scourged.
3. ...Jesus, who for us was crowned with thorns.
4. ...Jesus, who for us carried the heavy Cross.
5. ...Jesus, who for us was crucified.

III. "Clauses" for the Glorious Mysteries.
1. ...Jesus, who has risen from the dead.
2. ...Jesus, who has ascended into heaven.
3. ...Jesus, who has sent the Holy Spirit.
4. ...Jesus, who has taken you in body and soul into heaven.
5. ...Jesus, who has crowned you Queen of heaven and earth.

Prayers Before Mass

Dear Lord and Savior, I have come to your church to join together with your specially ordained priest and the other people present here, in offering the holy sacrifice of the Mass. Only the priest at the altar, ordained in the sacrament of holy orders, indelibly imprinted with the sacramental powers of your priesthood, O Christ Jesus, has the power of the twofold consecration to produce the victim of this sacrifice of the cross to be perpetuated here.

In this holy sacrifice of the Mass, about to be offered in this church in a few minutes, I shall be present at the renewal of your sacrifice of redemption. You, O Lord Jesus, shall not suffer a bloody, painful death again. In a mysterious but real way which I cannot understand by reason, but know by faith, the sacrifice of your death on the cross shall be offered here and now. I shall have a part in it.

You, O Christ, shall be the chief *priest* of this sacrifice, just as you were on the hill of Calvary. You, O Christ Jesus, shall be the *victim* of this sacrifice, just as you were on the cross. The same body, blood, soul and divinity there present and there offered, shall be here present and here offered and received in this holy Mass in which I am now about to participate.

I could no more truly be present at your sacrifice of the cross, dear Lord, than were I to be standing on the hill of Calvary as you offered yourself two thousand years ago. Now, *only the manner* of offering is different. Dear Lord, every time the Mass is celebrated, the work of our redemption is accomplished.

I have come here with a heart enkindled with faith and love. My faith is not as great as it could be. My love is not as complete as it should be. Lord, increase my faith and my love for a greater capacity so as to share in a greater fullness. I should celebrate each holy Mass with a greater faith and love than the Mass before.

Give me the grace, dear Lord, to offer you who are the immaculate victim, with great devotion, with great attention of mind and will. I wish to unite myself to your most Sacred Heart in that act with which you offered yourself long ago. I wish to have the dispositions of love and faith that filled the heart of your blessed Mother as she stood beneath the cross.

I wish to offer this holy Mass in reparation for all my past sins and the sins of the world. I wish to implore you, almighty God, for spiritual and temporal blessings. In and through this holy Mass, I ask that you bless holy Mother Church. Give her holy and worthy priests to offer your sacrifice and to preach your word.

Open my heart to receive your word, O Lord, in this liturgy of the word of God which will lead us, immediately, to the liturgy of the Eucharist.

Through this holy Mass, I ask you to bless all the members of my family, my relatives and friends. Keep them in your faith and love. Grant them salvation also through your word and your worship. Grant us all that we need in this life, for time and for eternity.

I believe that the liturgy of the Eucharist in this holy Mass will contain both the sacrifice and the sacrament of Jesus Christ. In the sacrament of holy communion, I shall receive the living body, blood, soul and divinity of my Lord and Savior, Jesus Christ. You will come to me, dear Lord, in all reality, not simply in sign. Living and substantial, real and true, dear Lord, you shall live in me and I shall live in you. By this holy sacrament you will grant me an increase in sanctifying grace. You shall increase your grace in my soul according to the dispositions of my heart. The greater the faith and love with which I approach the altar to receive you, the greater abundance will be the divine life you will then pour into my poor soul.

Lord, I am not worthy to receive you, now or ever. May my participation in the liturgy of the word of God and then in the liturgy of the Eucharist, flood my soul with greater faith and love, with better dispositions with which to receive you, dear Lord. May this sacrament make me aware of my union in Christ with other members of the Church. May this Mass and may this communion bear fruit in time and for eternity. Amen.

Prayers for After Mass

O heavenly Father, through the ministry of the priest of our Lord, Jesus Christ, in union with other members of the mystical body, the Church, I have offered the act of infinitely perfect adoration and thanksgiving. This is because you, Lord Jesus Christ, were the chief priest of the Mass in which I have just participated. I thank you, Lord God, for this privilege.

Jesus, help me to live the Mass. Help me to live the offering of self I have just made to God the Father, in the unity of the Holy Spirit, through you, Lord Jesus. My daily work, recreation, cares, pains have all been offered in, with and through you, Lord Jesus. The offering of my self was without value unaided. But joined to the perfect sacrifice, the victim which was you, Jesus, my offering of self united to you, made my offering pleasing to God my Father, and your Father. Without Jesus I can do nothing. Apart from him I am worth nothing. Christ Jesus, you give *value* to all that I am and all that I do.

During this holy Mass I have received into my heart, Jesus Christ, his sacred body and his precious blood together with his soul and divinity. "O sacrament most holy, O sacrament divine. All praise and all thanksgiving be every moment thine."

O Sacred Heart of Jesus, O eucharistic heart of Jesus, you are now within me with your heart beating with love for me and for all mankind. "Thy kingdom come." As long as the sacred species (consecrated bread) remains within me, I am most intimately united in a sacramental manner to the real presence of the God-Man. I cannot always have you within me sacramentally, dear Lord, but I can always be close to you by faith and by the increase of grace I have realized through this Mass and holy communion.

We adore you, O Christ, and we bless you, because by your holy cross you have redeemed the world.

Lord, I give you thanks for you have died upon the cross for my sins.

O Mary, my queen and my Mother, you are the Mother of the Church and the great woman of faith revealed in the sacred scriptures. Convey to me, through your intercession, the knowledge and the love of your Son, Jesus Christ. No one lived the Mass better

than you, O Virgin Mother. No one participated in the sacrifice of the cross more keenly
than you as you stood at the foot of the cross
on Calvary.

The apostle John, the young priest, took
you to his own and from his hands you received the living body of your Son. You exercised your great faith in the Mass as I must.
You exercised your faith at the foot of the
cross as you did during our Lord's years of
teaching, as he was growing into manhood
and during those years after the ascension. Intercede for me to live in faith the offering I
have made to our heavenly Father through
your Son in this sacrifice of the Mass.

Lord God, help me to remain always faithful to your teachings. I have heard your holy
word during this act of worship. Help me to
respond. I pray for your priests that they may
be true to you, reflect our Lord Jesus Christ in
their teachings and their lives. Their teachings
must be that of Christ for he said to his apostles: "He who hears you, hears me." I must
never form my holy Catholic faith except in
harmony with the teaching of the universal
Catholic Church. The magisterium — the
world's bishops united together with our holy
father, the pope — informs me of the voice of
Christ today. I must never follow mere opinions but this authentic faith of Christ Jesus.

Dear Lord, I offer you all my thoughts,

words, joys and actions of this week in union with the holy sacrifice of the Mass throughout the world. Amen.

Prayers After Holy Communion

(The following prayers are to suggest meditative prayers immediately after receiving holy communion. When many receive our Lord there may be time for private meditation, or the priest may go to the chair while the people meditate silently. If the people sing a common song of praise and thanksgiving it is well to join in the hymn in a prayerful manner. Some may wish to use these prayers after Mass, by remaining a few minutes.)

Dear Lord, you are now living in my soul with your body, blood, soul and divinity. Never in this life upon earth, could I be closer to you than I am now during these minutes after holy communion when you are sacramentally present within me. Only union with you in heaven could surpass the intimate union I now share in and with you, Lord Jesus.

My Jesus, I love you. I adore you. I place all my faith and all my trust in you. I am one with you. You are one with me. We are one together with all your other members in the mystical body, your holy Church. I have just received the sacrament of your unity whereby in this sacrament of love, you unite your brothers and sisters into one in yourself. You live in us. We are one in you, Lord Jesus Christ.

Now I can say in all truth and with its fullest meaning those words of the apostle Paul, "It is now no longer I who live but Christ who lives in me. . . . For me to live is Christ."

O Lord, you are light eternal. You are the light of the world and you share your light with and in us. May we share the light of your faith with others. We must not hide the light of your faith and love under a bushel basket, but let it shine forth for all to see.

The grace of this Mass, the grace of this holy communion, dear Lord, must shine forth to all with whom I come into contact this day, this week. I must witness your love, your person to everyone by the kind of person I am, by the kind of life I lead. May I always live in your love and never discredit the abundant graces you flood into my soul in this greatest of sacraments.

You have said, O Lord, "I have come that they may have life and have it more abundantly." You have said, dear Jesus, "I am life. . . ." Also, "Unless you eat the flesh of the Son of Man and drink his blood you shall not have life in you. . . . He who eats my flesh and drinks my blood has life everlasting and I will raise him up on the last day." Lord, these promises are now made to me as I have come to you in this sacrament and you have come to me. Amen.

Prayer to Our Lord Before An Image of the Crucifix

Look down upon me, good and gentle Jesus, while before your face I humbly kneel, and with burning soul pray and beseech you to fix deep in my heart lively sentiments of faith, hope and charity, true contrition for my sins and a firm purpose of amendment; while I contemplate with great love and tender pity your five wounds, pondering over them within me, and calling to mind the words which David, your prophet, said of you, my good Jesus: "They have pierced my hands and my feet; they have numbered all my bones."

(Say prayers for the holy father, the pope, e.g., Our Father, three Hail Marys, Glory be. . . .)

Prayer of St. Thomas Aquinas Following Holy Communion

I render you thanks, O holy Lord, Father almighty, eternal God, you who have deigned to feed me, a sinner and your unworthy servant — not for merits of my own but only through your mercy — with the precious body and blood of your Son, our Lord Jesus Christ.

I pray you that this holy communion may not be for my condemnation but for my pardon and salvation. May it be for me an armor of faith and a shield of good will. May it weaken my evil tendencies, root out from me concupiscence and lust, increase charity, patience, humility, obedience and all other virtues. May it mean for me a firm defense against the assaults of my enemies both visible and invisible, a perfect quieting of my impulses both carnal and spiritual, firm adherence to you, the one and true God and a blessed consummation at the end.

I pray you to lead me to that ineffable banquet where you with your Son and the Holy Spirit are to your saints true light, the fullness of beatitude, everlasting joy, the culmination of delight and perfect happiness. Through the same Christ our Lord. Amen.

Anima Christi of St. Ignatius

Soul of Christ, sanctify me.
Body of Christ, save me.
Blood of Christ, inebriate me.
Water from the side of Christ, wash me.

Passion of Christ, strengthen me.
O good Jesus, hear me.
Within your wounds hide me.
Permit me not to be separated from you.
From the malignant enemy defend me.
In the hour of my death call me.
And bid me come to you.
That, with your saints, I may praise you.
Forever and ever. Amen.

Confession—
The Sacrament of Penance

(This sacrament of God's mercy was given to us on the evening of the first Easter Sunday when Jesus said to his apostles [the first priests]: "Receive the Holy Spirit, whose sins you shall forgive, they are forgiven them; and whose sins you shall retain, they are retained" [John 20, 23]. In every sacrament the very person of Christ Jesus is present and acts, and so it is in confession. If an individual is in mortal sin a good confession is required before receiving our Lord in holy communion. But the good Catholic should avail himself of this sacrament frequently because of the special graces it affords the soul.

(To make a good confession the following conditions are required: Sorrow for sin; a firm intention to strive to avoid sin in the future; a

willingness to perform the penance the priest gives us so as to make satisfaction for the temporal punishment due to our forgiven sins; telling our sins to the priest including their number and circumstances [this is strictly required for mortal sin and recommended for venial sin]; and an examination of conscience.

(To help you examine your conscience, you may use the following guides according to your state in life.)

Prayers Before Confession

Heavenly Father, I have sinned against you. I am not worthy to be your child. You are all good and I am sinful. Through your infinite mercy and the love of the Sacred Heart of your Son, Jesus Christ, I beg forgiveness in this holy sacrament of penance which I am now going to receive. You have promised, merciful Savior, that you would forgive me my sins unto an unlimited number provided that I was truly sorry for them. I have sinned against your love again, dear Jesus, and I am sorry because I fear the punishment which my sins deserve. But most especially, dear Lord, I want to be sorry for them because my offenses have been against your love.

Most Holy Spirit, infinite source of light and love, grant me the gift of sorrow based on the love of Jesus Christ. Help me to know my sins and to be truly sorry for them. It was my sins too, that caused the extreme sufferings of Jesus in his agony in the garden; the blood and sweat, because he was sorrowful unto death as he beheld my sins and those of the world. It was my sins too, that caused him to be scourged at the pillar. I had a part in making that cross heavy for my Savior and nailing him to it where he suffered untold sufferings while he thirsted for my salvation.

The penance the priest will give me will be but little of the penance I should do for my sins. I wish to spend the future, not only striving by the help of your grace, dear Lord, to avoid sin, but in growing in the love of the Sacred Heart and in doing penance for my past failings. I implore the love of the Immaculate Heart of Mary to obtain for me from her Son the dispositions I need for a good confession. I implore also my good angel, and all the saints and angels, to unite with me in thanking and praising Jesus for this opportunity to confess my sins and obtain forgiveness from his merciful love.

Examination of Conscience
For Men and Women

My Prayer Life:
Have I been a person of daily prayer? Has

my failure to be a person of prayer been the cause of weakness of faith and its practice in my daily life? Is my faith a living faith which I have not hesitated to show in ordinary events of daily life? Do I take the lead in seeing that there is prayer in my family life? Do I pass up opportunities for growth in faith and love? (E.g., visits to the most blessed sacrament; some special parish or family devotion.)

Did I participate in the sacrifice of the Mass every Sunday and holy day? Did I try to rationalize away this serious obligation? Did I retain a spirit of individualism in public worship? Did I try to participate according to my ability in the singing, responses, the Eucharist?

Did I listen prayerfully to the sermon? Was I unduly inattentive or critical? Deliberately come late, leave Mass early?

Do I have any kind of a spiritual program in my life other than Sunday Mass?

(A spiritual program should consist of some plan of daily and weekly prayer and spiritual reading.)

Is there an overflow of my prayer life into my life in the world so that men can recognize that I am a Christian?

My Life in the Community:

Do I love all men, regardless of race or color, and do I put this love into practice to the extent that I am able in my state of life?

How did I treat my neighbors? Was I kind, respectful, friendly to everyone or only to those who naturally appealed to me? Did I respect the property of others? Did I make restitution for property stolen or destroyed? Was I *honest* in all my dealings with others? In conversation? In all business transactions?

Have I given a day's work for a day's pay? Was I just in relationships to those who work under me? Do I demand my rights without consideration for that of others? Is my business run according to Christian influences?

Have I contributed to the Church and other charitable causes according to my honest means? Can I see no need to be charitable to causes at a distance? Did I make other contributions to the Church and community in general by contributing my services of labor? Did I strive to bring Christian principles into decisions of groups in my community?

Have I used my tongue to harm another's reputation? Make restitution? Did I use my tongue irreverently by bad language? Stories, jokes? Occasion of sin to others? Did I drive so as to endanger the lives and safety of others? Did I abuse the use of liquor and try to justify my abuses?

Respect for Authority:
Do I criticize authority in the presence of children and youth? Do I respect and support

the authority of Church, government, school?
As a parent am I permissive, refusing to exercise my God-given authority with consistency, firmness and love? Am I just in administering or accepting authority? Have I been jealous of others in the exercise of authority?

Family Life:

Is my family environment truly a Catholic Christian home? Do I encourage prayer in my children? Do we say family prayers each day? Do I pay any attention to the religious education of my children or completely entrust it to others? Am I truly the primary religious educator of my child? Does a spirit of penance characterize our family observances of Fridays and Lent?

Do I teach my children proper reverence and behavior in Church? Do I fulfill my role as a parent in disciplining children? Do we support one another in discipline? Do I leave all discipline to my spouse?

Am I so occupied with my work that I forget to give time and attention to my children? Do I spend any time with them, respecting each one as a person with individual needs? Do I teach my children Christian values in life? Do I scandalize my children by word or act? With my older children do I show patience, understanding, for their developing personalities?

Is there opportunity for good Catholic reading in our home?

Do I understand love in a spirit of sacrifice and giving of self? Is my love more a self-centeredness? Do I try to view sex according to God's plan? *If married,* have I deliberately practiced artificial birth control? Have I tried to rationalize away the Church's official teachings on the use of sex, permitting the world's way and opinion to form my conscience rather than Christ who said to his Church, "He who hears you, hears me"? Have I sought out a priest who I thought might agree with my point of view or that of the world, rather than seeking truth itself in a true conscience? Have I been unfaithful to my spouse? Encouraged advances from others? What was the cause of my unfaithfulness? Did I contribute to my spouse's infidelity? *If unmarried,* have I encouraged advances, passions? Fornication? Any impure acts alone, with another? Have I tried to justify free love? What does God's word say? Have I dated a divorced person? Am I immodest in dress, action?

Do I supervise family entertainment — TV, movies, reading?

Do I occasionally encourage the family to participate in the sacraments?

Am I understanding and forgiving of the faults of my spouse? Do I try to encourage my spouse in moments of trial and frustration? Do

I build on my spouse's good points or tear them down?

Apostolic Christianity:

Have I been a source of encouragement to priests and religious? Have I caused disunity in the parish? Do I look to the Church only to receive, not to give? Do I criticize the Church while making no positive contributions? Do I strive to bring others closer to Christ? Am I indifferent about the salvation of others? Am I concerned about the poor, the oppressed? What do I personally do for these? Do I realize that I too, am the Church? Do I pray for or merely criticize those who have given scandal? Am I honest, open and humble in discussing my problems with my confessor?

Am I doing my share to preach the gospel to every creature and spread the Church to the ends of the earth as our Lord commanded?

(Recite the "Act of Contrition" from your heart before entering the confessional.)

Examination of Conscience For Young People

My Prayer Life:

Do I follow our Lord's desire to "pray always"? Is there *daily* prayer in my life? Any spiritual program on a daily or weekly basis? Have I tried to rationalize away the Lord's commandment and that of his Church about keeping the Lord's day holy? Do I think my personal form of prayer is as good as the perfect worship which Jesus Christ himself gives in perpetuating his sacrifice of the cross in every holy Mass? Am I conscious that while at Mass, I am united in and to the person of Jesus Christ in renewing his perfect act of worship of Calvary, made present again? Is my faith a *living faith?* Is there an overflow of my prayer life into my daily living? Does my reception of the Lord's body and blood in holy communion affect my daily living? Do I enter into singing, responses at Mass in a spirit of unity with God's people? Is there depth to my Christianity?

Home Life:

Do I respect the authority of my parents? Do I too easily assume that they are out of pace with the modern world, not informed, give them no credit for the wisdom of experience? Hold grudges? Prompt to contribute to work around home? Obedient, cheerful, kind, friendly? Do I push younger family members around? Am I irritable, sulky at home? Do I show respect for relatives, older people? Do I willingly participate in home religious practices? Do I resent my parents' interest in my salvation and company-keeping? Have I been open and honest with my parents?

Community:

Do I think only of my own interests or am I considerate of others? Do I consider the feelings of friends, neighbors, teachers? Do I limit my kindnesses to a close circle? Do I work the attitudes of others against the authority of teacher, priest, law official? Do I tear down others rather than accept responsibility and grow in maturity? Did I contribute to destruction of property directly or by silent observance? Did I cheat in school work? Neglect study of subjects, including religion? Did I look down upon others of a different color or poorer circumstances? Have I been jealous? Have I given generous consideration to the serving of God and God's people as a priest or a religious? Have I been *honest* in all my dealings with others? In conversation? In all transactions, business or otherwise?

Purity:

Is my mentality about sex formed by the plan of God and the authentic teachings of his Church, or by the world, trashy publications and movies? Is it influenced by others with warped mentalities? Have I committed impure actions with my body alone? Have I committed an impure action with another? Have I confessed such sins according to number and circumstances, or vaguely so the confessor misses of what I have been guilty? Have I tried to justify "free love" by false opinions rather than form my conscience according to God's word? Do I shop around for a priest who might agree or be easy on me, rather than seek the will of God to correct my ways and live in God's good grace? Have I led another into sin? Do I try to conquer habits of impurity by praying in times of temptation, not being self-centered, receiving the sacraments frequently? Do I unnecessarily delay my confession when I need God's help and forgiveness? Did I go to holy communion when I should have gone to confession first? Did I needlessly entertain impure thoughts and desires? Jokes? Stories? Was I immodest in dress? Did I date a person who is a danger to my faith? Did I date someone I could never marry, such as a divorced person?

Personal Relationship to God:

Do I observe Friday as a day of penance? Lent as a season of penance? Do I use food and drink in moderation? Do I rationalize use of drink or drugs? Do I have Christian attitudes about dating? Do I pray for and seek a partner in courtship who could help me and as a possible future family live a Christian life and get to heaven? Am I proud? Do I strive to control my emotions? Have I honestly asked myself in God's presence whether he may have a special vocation for me in the Church?

Apostolic Christianity:

Have I been a source of encouragement to priests and religious? Have I caused disunity in the parish? Do I look to the Church only to receive, not to give? Do I criticize the Church while making no positive contributions? Do I strive to bring others closer to Christ? Am I indifferent about the salvation of others? Am I concerned about the poor, the oppressed? What do I personally do for these? Do I seek my vocation in life in a self-centered way, or how I can best contribute to the betterment of the world, its salvation and my own? Do I realize that I too am the Church? Do I pray for or merely criticize those who have given scandal? Am I honest, open and humble in discussing my problems with my confessor?

(Recite the "Act of Contrition" from your heart before entering the confessional.)

Prayer to the
Sacred Heart of Jesus

O Sacred Heart of Jesus, burning with love for me, I desire to love you more and more. You are all good and I am weak and lowly. My sins have too often offended you. Yet, dear Jesus, your loving mercy is always waiting for me to return. You even seek after me when I am in sin.

I find it so hard to forgive others, dear Jesus. Your Sacred Heart finds no difficulty at all in forgiving my sins and those of all mankind if we but approach your infinite ocean of mercy.

O Sacred Heart, font of love and mercy, it was your great love that gave yourself to us in the most blessed sacrament. Your eucharistic heart is always present in our tabernacles. You renew the sacrifice of your great love in every holy Mass. I am so cold and so ungrateful and do not return to you, O Sacred Heart of Jesus, the love that you have for me. I am sorry. Forgive me and help me to do better.

Give me the grace to make you loved more and more. May I honor your sacred image. May I spread the knowledge of your love to others. May I find a safe refuge in you at the moment of death.

O Sacred Heart of Jesus, I put my trust in You. O Sacred Heart of Jesus, I give you my heart and my soul. O Sacred Heart of Jesus, make me love you more and more. All for you, most Sacred Heart of Jesus. Your kingdom come. Amen.

Prayer to the Sorrowful and Immaculate Heart of Mary

O Immaculate Heart of Mary, how favored you were to be the chosen one of God so as to become his Mother. Because God has destined you to be his Mother, he preserved you free of original sin from the very first moment of your conception. You were never touched by the slightest sin during your entire life upon earth. You are the immaculate conception. O Mary, conceived without sin, pray for us who have recourse to you.

Immaculate Heart of Mary, your precious heart beats for love of me and all your spiritual children. You are truly my Mother and my queen. As Mother of the Church, it is your greatest desire to have all men upon earth come to the knowledge and the love of the true faith of your Son. You truly have a Mother's heart. When I hurt the Sacred Heart of your Son by sin, you too feel the hurt, and the sword pierces your Immaculate Heart, as thorns of sin pierce his heart aflame with love.

Mary, you who pondered the word of God in your heart so often upon earth, bring me and all mankind to deep faith and its practice. Grant peace to a world not able to obtain it of its own power. The Sacred Heart of Jesus has entrusted the peace of the world into your hands. Queen of peace, Immaculate Heart of

Mary, hail Mary, full of grace, pray for us now and at the hour of our death. Amen.

Prayer of a Sick Person

Almighty and eternal God, I offer you my sickness in union with the sufferings your Son endured when he was upon earth. The sacred body of Jesus was inflicted with untold sufferings. His pains were intense and you willed that he suffer in such a manner for the salvation of the world. By uniting my sufferings to those of Jesus, I can make them meritorious unto my salvation and that of others.

In your mercy, O Sacred Heart of Jesus, grant me the strength to accept my infirmity, and if it be your will, may I speedily be restored to health. You, dear Lord, who cured the mother-in-law of Peter, grant that I too may be cured so as to resume my daily duties. If not, give me the humility to accept the help of others and the grace to see your kind and gracious purpose working in all the events of my life. Amen.

Prayer for
Resignation of Will

Dear God, there are many things in life I cannot change. Give me the grace to accept them and the strength to change the things I can with your help. I know, dear God, that you will do nothing but what is for my salvation and that of others and for your honor and glory. I know that the longest life upon earth is but short in comparison with eternity. All that is important is that I get to heaven. If I do that with the grace of Jesus Christ, nothing else matters. If I do not accomplish that, nothing else matters.

As you hung upon the cross, dear Jesus, it was not easy for you to say to your heavenly Father, "Your will be done." In this affliction of mine that weighs me down so heavily, may I joyfully look upwards to the divine will of God, united with the Sacred Heart, and utter, "Your will be done. . . . Your kingdom come." Amen.

Prayer for a Soul In Danger of Death
(To be said at the side of the dying person)

O most merciful heart of Jesus, I beg you to grant grace to this soul whom you love, to unite his (her) will to yours as you suffered your agony in the garden. Wash away with your most precious blood all the sins this poor soul has ever committed and for which he (she) fears there may still be guilt.

Make his (her) sufferings meritorious unto salvation. He (she) wishes to pray in this manner: O almighty God, lover of souls in Christ Jesus, I give you my body and soul for time and for eternity. Forgive me all the sins that I have ever committed. I am sorry. I love you. I believe that your divine Son became man and died for my sins. I believe that you can save me by the blood of the cross. I believe that there are three Persons in one God, Father, Son and Holy Spirit. I trust in you, Lord Jesus, to save me. I want your blessed Mother Mary to pray for me now and at the hour of my death. I ask the prayers of my guardian angel and all the angels and saints, and especially of my patron saint. Lord Jesus, grant me eternal salvation that I may be with you forever in the eternal bliss of my heavenly home. Amen.

Prayer for Civil Authorities

Lord God, grant to the president of the United States, to the congress, and to all law officials on the national, state and local levels, wisdom and justice, the gifts of counsel and fortitude, to conduct your affairs and that of men with righteousness. May they realize that all authority comes from God and use it as your representatives. May men respect all lawful authority justly exercised.

May our governing officials bring us to true peace and a prosperity that will be unto our eternal salvation. Amen.

The Gap Prayer
(Prayer for understanding others of different views, ages, cultures, races)

Lord of the ages, Lord of the nations, Lord God almighty, give me a heart to understand others' point of view. Widen my vision beyond the narrow confines of my little world to embrace the horizons of knowledge and love that span all boundaries.

There is no man or woman, no teen-ager, no child, from whom I cannot learn something. Each person, young or old, black or white, yellow or red, is a unique creation of God. And Lord, the God of love, you made each one of us with our unique personality, with unique bodily characteristics, because you loved us. And to each one of us you have said, "I have loved you with an everlasting love."

God, you talk to us in everything and in everyone. The beauty of your world which tells of your existence and your power, we sometimes mar with our excessive living and our uncharitableness toward other persons created in your own image and likeness. Lord, deliver me from polluting the beauty of your world and the gifts of your creation. Lord, spare me from failing to see you in the face of every man, woman and child that I shall ever meet.

Too often, dear Lord, we do not recognize you in the goodness of your creation. We fail to see you in the faces of certain people because their skin is colored different from our own. We are more blind than the blind, who in their love for one another are not bothered by the color of skin.

Too often, dear Lord, I do not appreciate the view of one that is older. His vision may be deeper and wider than my own. Too often, dear Lord, I do not comprehend the view of one who is younger. His vision is fresher, bolder, more courageous than my own.

Too often, dear Lord, I do not appreciate the view and the custom of one whose culture is different from mine. Different cultures penetrate your goodness and beauty, your wisdom and knowledge, from angles I have never seen or known. I could learn to know and to love more from cultures of others. Instead, dear Lord, I recognize your beauty and your goodness in limited color, in restricted goodness and narrow views.

Help me, God of love, to blend your

freshness and fortitude in youth with your wisdom and experience in age. Help me recognize the fuller beauty of your Persons in persons of various colors. Bless me, dear Lord, with a knowledge and a love that is tempered by age, wisdom, culture and you, God, in Christ Jesus, who are all things to all men. Amen.

Prayer for Peace
(St. Francis of Assisi)

Lord, make me an instrument of your peace;
Where there is hatred, let me sow love;
Where there is injury, pardon;
Where there is discord, union;
Where there is doubt, faith;
Where there is despair, hope;
Where there is darkness, light;
And where there is sadness, joy.
O divine master, grant that I may not
so much seek to be consoled as to console;
To be understood, as to understand;
To be loved, as to love;
For it is in giving that we receive.
It is in pardoning that we are pardoned,
And it is in dying that we are born
to eternal life.

Prayer Before Making a Decision

Lord, I have an important decision to make. (Name it. . . .) I seek your wisdom in making the right choice that will be for my good and that of others in both time and in eternity. You have said in your Son, Jesus Christ, "Ask and you shall receive." I ask for the grace and the wisdom to choose that which is according to your will.

Too often what seems best to man, is not best for his salvation according to the mind of God. God's ways and thoughts are so elevated above our own. If I cannot always see clearly your way, O God, or understand the wisdom of the events you permit and cause to come into my life, permit me at least to trust in you. Help me to pray as though all depended on You, dear Lord, and to work as though all depended upon myself. In this way I will use the talents you have given me and give credit to the outcome as in harmony with your divine will. Teach me always to seek your will before my own.

Come, Holy Spirit, fill the hearts of your faithful and enkindle in them the fire of your love. Send forth your spirit and they shall be created and you shall renew the face of the earth.

O God, who does instruct the hearts of the faithful, by the light of the Holy Spirit, grant us by the same Spirit to be truly wise and ever to rejoice in his consolation through the same Christ our Lord. Amen.

Prayer Before Traveling

Lord, direct me in the way of peace and safety. May my traveling be unto your glory. May it be a help unto my salvation.

God has given his angel charge over me to keep me in all his ways. Angel of God, appointed to be my guardian, through your intercession enlighten my way, protect me on this journey in every way.

O God, you gave the blessed archangel Raphael unto your servant Tobias to be his fellow traveler. Grant unto me the protection of the same that he may keep me and shield me, help and defend me. Bring me back home, dear Lord, safe in mind, body and soul. Amen.

Prayer of a Mass Server Before Mass

Lord Jesus, it is my privilege to serve at your holy altar. I am not serving simply for the man who is your priest. It is you yourself I serve at the altar, dear Lord. You, Christ Jesus, will be the chief priest and victim of this holy sacrifice of the Mass.

During this holy Mass in which I shall participate in a most intimate way, you, dear Lord, will renew the sacrifice of the cross. You will become present on the altar with your body, blood, soul and divinity. Make me as worthy as possible to serve at your altar. Keep me in the state of grace. Make me always conscious in all my behavior that I am your altar boy chosen to serve you in a special way.

Prayer of a Mass Server After Mass

Thank you, dear Lord, for the great privilege of serving at your altar. I have just participated in the greatest act possible upon earth. As it were, I have stood and knelt at the foot of the cross on Calvary. I have been present as you offered to the heavenly Father your great act of love and redemption. Next to the priest at the altar, I had the greatest part in this sacred offering in your name, Lord Jesus.

O Jesus, grant that I shall always be worthy to serve you in a fitting manner. May what I have done this day, at this altar, carry over into my daily actions. May I live this Mass in thought, word and deed. May I always remember to come to your altar, prepared to receive you and serve you in the state of sanctifying grace. May I remember to approach you in the sacrament of penance, from time to time.

Help me, dear Lord, to know what you want of me in life. Speak, Lord, your servant is listening. Amen.

Prayer of a Lector Before Mass

Lord Jesus, I have been chosen to stand in your sanctuary and announce your sacred word. This is a high office and brings with it a serious responsibility. I am to be your spokesman today. Whenever the scriptures are read in church, you, dear Lord, are present in your word and speaking to your people. In this holy sacrifice of the Mass, you will use me, Lord Jesus, as your instrument in announcing your sacred word.

Lord God, if I am to be in some small but mighty way, the instrument of your word, I must be an upright Catholic in word and in deed. Your holy word must be reflected in the kind of life I lead. I must be a witness to your word, not only by pronouncing it in letter but by living it in spirit. Help me, dear Lord, to be more worthy of this office entrusted to me. Amen.

Prayer of a Young Person Not Going to Mass

Lord, why should I go to "plastic Masses"? Lord, why should I go to Mass when I get nothing out of it? Your people seem so non-responsive. The message of your priest does not apply to my life or the needs of the times. I cannot put my heart into it and feel dishonest pretending. Lord, am I not doing right? Am I not just as good a Catholic practicing my faith in this manner?

Lord, I'll ask myself again the meaning of the Mass. It is your sacrifice of the cross perpetuated. It matters not if the language be in Hebrew, Greek, Latin or English. I should go to Mass not to get, but to give. The giving is the gift of myself and I am nothing. United to the victim-gift of the sacrifice which is Christ Jesus, my nothingness is transformed so that my person becomes one with the Person of Jesus. Have I been going to get a thrill, to be turned on? Or has it been to give God the Father his Son, whose sacrifice is renewed at every Mass? And my life is given too. It is swallowed up in Christ's giving of himself.

Lord, if the message is not to my liking, if

it is not what I want to hear, was not this true of many who listened to you in Jesus years ago? Should I be telling you or your representatives what I should hear? Is there not something to be gained from your word in the scriptures of every Mass? You are present in your word at every Mass. You are present in your sacrifice and you are present in your sacramental body and blood with your soul and divinity at every sacrifice of the Mass. No dynamic presentation can make these more real. Is your Mass really plastic, Lord? Or am I the one whose artificiality, whose pretense, is keeping me away?

Prayer for the Poor Souls

God, hear the prayers I send forth for the suffering souls in purgatory. They are my friends and they are your friends. They can no longer help themselves, but I can, by my prayers, good works, my sacrifices on their behalf. I want to pray for all the poor souls in purgatory and I want at this time to remember especially (name[s]). Dear God, have mercy on those who suffer in the fires of purgatory. They died in your love and in the faith of your Son, Jesus Christ.

While not in the state of perfection at

their death, dear Lord, while dying with venial sins on their souls, or not having made full satisfaction for the temporal punishment due to their forgiven mortal and venial sins, yet, dear Lord, they did repent of all serious sin before death. They did die in the state of grace. I thank you that you grant the faithful departed the opportunity to make full satisfaction after death for their failures in life. If my salvation depended upon a state of perfection and if I died at this moment, I am aware of what my fate would be.

Dear Lord, you have revealed that nothing defiled shall enter heaven. A soul could not bear to stand in your all-holy and pure presence with the slightest defilement of soul. In your loving mercy you have granted us the cleansing fires of purgatory. And yet these souls suffer intensely in your love. They burn with desire to be perfectly united with you. I pray for their speedy deliverance and ask for them, the intercession of your most blessed Mother and all the angels and saints. May the angels which guarded them in life upon earth, now pray for their speedy deliverance.

I offer you, dear God, the most precious blood of your Son, Jesus Christ, on behalf of these suffering souls in purgatory. I offer you the Masses in which I participate and in union with the holy sacrifice of the Mass throughout the world.

Eternal rest grant unto them, O Lord, and let perpetual light shine upon them; may the souls of the faithful departed through the mercy of God, rest in peace. Amen.

Prayer of the Elderly And Shut-In

Dear God, my days are long and yet they are short in number that I shall spend upon this earth. It is difficult to accept your will at times and yet I know that your will is unto my salvation and your glory. I am not able to get around, meet people and work, like it would be my will. Yet not my will, but yours, be done.

When you hung upon the cross, when you spent the night in prison after men arrested you in the garden, dear Jesus, you too, could not move around with your human body as others. You submitted to the will of the heavenly Father. I unite my trials, my long hours, to the patience and sufferings which you endured when you were upon earth. I desire that these days upon earth, every one of them, be unto my salvation and that of others. Of myself, my trials are without merit. United to yours, to your Sacred Heart, my sufferings, endurances, even my very heartbeats, can become meritorious.

This earth is not my true and lasting home. Heaven is my home. I thank you, dear God, for every day, for every hour you give me upon this earth. By living each hour in your love, I can grow in your grace and glorify you and have a more intimate place with you in heaven for all eternity. I long for the day which will begin my eternity, when I shall behold you face-to-face, even as you are. I long for the loving embrace of the Sacred Heart and that of the Immaculate Heart of Mary. I look forward with loving anticipation to see all the angels and saints and loved ones who have gone before me. Your kingdom come. Amen.

Prayer of a Priest
After His Mass
(Pope Pius X)

I beseech you, O Lord Jesus Christ, that your passion may be strength to fortify, shield and defend me; your wounds food and drink to feed, inebriate and delight me. May the sprinkling of your blood wash away all my sins; your death be unending life; your cross eternal glory. In these be my refreshment and joy, health and sweetness of heart, who lives and reigns, world without end. Amen.

Eucharistic Offering
(From the Imitation of Christ, IV, 9)

O Lord, to whom belongs all that is in heaven and earth, I desire to consecrate myself wholly unto you and to be yours forevermore. This day do I offer myself unto you, O Lord, in singleness of heart, to serve and obey you always, and I offer you without ceasing a sacrifice of praise and thanksgiving. Receive me, O my Savior, in union with the holy oblation of your precious blood which I offer unto you this day, in the presence of angels, that this sacrifice may avail unto my salvation and that of the whole world.

An Offering of Self
(From the spiritual exercises of St. Ignatius of Loyola)

Take, O Lord, into your hands my entire liberty, my memory, my understanding and my will. All that I am and have, you have given me, and I surrender them to you, to be so disposed in accordance with your holy will.

Give me your love and your grace; with these I am rich enough and desire nothing more.

Act of Resignation
(Pope Pius X)

O Lord, my God, from this moment do I accept from your hands, with a quiet and trusting heart, whatsoever death you shall choose to send me, with its pains and griefs.

Visit to the Most Blessed Sacrament

Dear Jesus, I believe that you are really and truly substantially present in the tabernacle before me under the appearance of bread. The sanctuary lamp burns in honor of your real presence in this Catholic church. I love and adore you profoundly and beg pardon for those who do not love you and do not adore your presence in this most blessed sacrament.

I kneel in your presence, unworthy as I am, and beg pardon for all the offenses I and others have committed against you. Warm our cold hearts. Grant us peace and happiness in the knowledge that your abiding love made it possible for us to receive you in holy communion and to adore you in this most august sacrament.

O eucharistic heart of Jesus, I adore you profoundly. Let the love of your Sacred Heart radiate the warmth of its fire to enkindle my own poor cold heart. Enlighten the darkness of my mind. Strengthen the weakness of my will. Bathe me in your most precious blood which I now offer to our heavenly Father in union with the holy sacrifice of the Mass being offered throughout the world.

You know, dear Lord Jesus, that I am here present before you. You can read the desires of my heart. You know my problems, my petitions, my ingratitude. Accept at least my weak desire to love you more and may I never offend you. Amen.

Prayer of Spouses For Each Other

Blessed Mother Mary and St. Joseph, by your intercession, obtain for me and my spouse an understanding love for each other. You were both persons of faith and love. You knew suffering and joy. Your trials were great. St. Joseph, you trusted Mary even when you did not know the source of her conception. You were a just man in all things. Holy Mary, your great disposition of faith, pondering the words of Jesus in your heart, led you and your spouse always to live in faith and trust in the

Lord in all the many trials and difficulties you encountered.

When the life of your child was in danger, Mary and Joseph, you had to leave your home and flee to a strange land. You went seeking your child sorrowfully when he became separated from you as he approached his adolescent years. Mary, you knew the pain of separation when Joseph died in your arms and you and Jesus carried on and you sorrowfully witnessed the conflicts Jesus met with the world of his time. It was your faith in the Lord, your trust in one another that sustained you in every difficulty of married life. Obtain for me and my spouse that same faith and trust.

Dear God, grant us the grace to live with one another in peace and harmony until death do us part. May we bear with one another's weaknesses and strengthen one another's good qualities. Help us to forgive one another's failings. Grant us patience, kindness, cheerfulness and a spirit of placing the welfare of one another ahead of self. Through Jesus Christ, your only Son, our Lord. Amen.

Prayer for a Priestly Heart
(St. Thomas Aquinas)

Give me, O Lord, an ever-watchful heart

which no subtle speculation may ever lure from you.

Give me a noble heart that no unworthy affection shall ever draw downwards to earth.

Give me a heart of honesty that no insincerity shall warp.

Give me a heart of courage that no distress shall ever crush or quench.

Give me a heart so free that no perverted or impetuous affection shall ever claim it for its own.

Prayer of a Priest Before Mass

Lord Jesus, I am not worthy to approach your altar. I am to be your chief representative at this holy sacrifice of the Mass. Your very Person shall act in and through my poor ministry. When I was ordained in the sacrament of holy orders, the Holy Spirit descended from heaven and imprinted upon my soul the indelible character of you, Lord Jesus Christ, for all eternity. I shall be a priest forever. No power upon earth or in heaven will ever change that. At my words, which are your words, "This is my body . . . this is my blood," you, dear Lord, shall become present upon the altar under the forms of bread and wine. At this action you shall perpetuate your sacrifice of the cross. Your glorified and risen body, blood, soul and divinity shall be present. As the representative of you, the good shepherd, I shall feed your flock with you, dear Jesus. I shall receive you into my own heart and soul. Purify my soul and all evil desires. Make my heart like unto yours.

No man upon earth is worthy of such an exalted office. But hundreds and thousands of people depend upon my cooperating with your grace which shall always be sufficient for me. You give no office in life without at the same time giving all the help needed to perform it fittingly. I trust in you, O Sacred Heart of Jesus. I shall now approach your altar. Keep me conscious throughout this infinite act of worship that your great sacrifice is now being offered. Amen.

A Farmer's Prayer

Dear God, make our fields and pastures fertile and bless the labor of our hands. Grant us seasonable rains and bring us an abundant harvest. May we see your power, your goodness and your beauty reflected in the daily growth and development of the products of the land. May we always realize our total dependence upon you, almighty God, that whereas we may plant, only you can give the growth. You, dear God, are the chief farmer and may our cooperation with your daily work bring mankind daily bread and closer to you.

Dear God, bestow justice in fair prices for our products and our labors. Grant us the spirit of working together with fellow farmers to dignify farm life and to assure the continuance of the family farm. May I always look at others' views and efforts with an understanding heart of charity.

May we, dear Lord, farm in such a way as to preserve your lands of which we are stewards. The power and the beauty which you have placed in the soil must remain for future generations. I shall strive to realize that I am but a pilgrim passing through this world briefly on my way to heaven. In some way, by your strength and grace, I shall strive to leave this world a little better for future generations. Amen.

A Laboring Man's Prayer

Dear God, all labor of the body, I realize, has dignity. Whether I work in mine or factory, in store or any other type of labor, I work in union with your people and in harmony with the gifts of this world which you have created. By working in various phases of industry, men united in various vocations of life, I must realize, glorify you, almighty God, and help one another.

Help me, dear God, to be conscientious to give a day's work for a day's pay. May I respect the property of others for whom I work. May I put forth effort with a personal interest. May my spirit of charity contribute to the happiness at work of my employer and fellow employees.

May I have you, St. Joseph, as the patron of the workingman. You taught the boy Jesus to work with his hands and to work with others. May I be generous in sharing my knowledge of work with others and may I be humble in learning from others unto the profit of us all and unto the glory of God. Amen.

A Professional Worker's Prayer

Dear God, you have called me to a vocation in life that involves labor of a professional nature. My skill took special training. You gave me the talent for this profession and I depended upon the learning and instruction of others to develop it. Now that I find myself engaged in this profession, I must not abuse the powers that are mine and take advantage of others whose skill or training is not in my line.

Dear God, I shall have to answer one day for every client who has employed my services. May I reflect your kindness, wisdom, understanding, prudence unto the growth of others in your likeness and unto my own salvation.

May I be open and honest, sharing my knowledge with others, so that they, together with me, may grow in the likeness of your Son, Jesus Christ. Amen.

Prayer for Religious Sisters and Brothers

Dear Jesus, give strength to your consecrated sisters and brothers to persevere in their religious vocation and to the sacred vows they have taken. They are consecrated to you by poverty, chastity and obedience. Yet they are human and subjected to the same temptations as is all mankind.

Help your religious, dear Lord, to remain faithful to the holy Church and be that example to one another and to all the faithful which will inspire greater effort to grow into the likeness of Christ Jesus, their spouse. Give them humility, generosity, kindness, honesty even with themselves. Help them to realize that in their teachings of faith, they are to represent you, as the voice of the Church is your voice, O Lord. They are to teach you, present your voice, not the mere opinion of men.

Give them courage, O Lord, when others seem to reject your calling. I ask you to bless and strengthen all religious but especially those who have been dear to me, those who taught me, guided me, comforted me when I was sick, those whose good example have led me to a Catholic way of life. I wish to remember especially (name[s]).

Almighty God, keep your sisters and brothers especially close to the Sacred Heart of Jesus and under the intercessory care of the Immaculate Heart of Mary. Keep them true to you, dear God, until their souls rest securely in your eternal embrace in heaven. Amen.

The Memorare
(St. Bernard)

Remember, O most gracious Virgin Mary, that never was it known that anyone who fled to your protection, implored your help or sought your intercession was left unaided. Inspired with this confidence, I fly to you, O Virgin of virgins, my Mother. To you I come, before you I stand sinful and sorrowful. O Mother of the word incarnate, do not ignore my petitions but in your mercy hear and answer me. Amen.

Morning Prayers

Dear Lord, you have brought me to the light of day. I desire to spend this day with you in union with your all-holy will. Keep me from sin. Help me grow in grace so that I shall have a happier and more intimate place in heaven with you and your blessed Mother, St. Joseph, all the angels and saints because of this day, and every day, which I shall spend upon earth.

If I should come to the end of my life upon earth this day, dear Lord, I pray that my guardian angel shall be able to present my soul in your sight, holy and pure, without serious sin, and worthy at least for the final cleansing fires of purgatory. I wish to offer the prayers and good works of this day in reparation for all my past sins and the temporal punishments due to them. I wish to gain all the indulgences which Mother Church has attached to any prayers and good works I may perform this day.

Help me, dear Jesus, to witness your Person, your love, this day to all whom I may meet. Give me the courage to live my Catholic Christian faith in every situation and never be

ashamed to profess you openly. Your kingdom come. Amen.

*(Add "Morning Offering" and any other
prayers of your choosing found in this prayer
book.)*

Night Prayers

Thank you, dear God, for the graces of
this day. I have not served you perfectly and
yet you have preserved me and protected me
unto this moment. I renew the offering I made
of my total self this morning. I offer you too
whatever sins I have committed this day that
they may be washed away in the most precious blood of my Lord and Savior, Jesus
Christ.

*(Examine your conscience over failings of
the days.)*

(What caused them?)

(How can I avoid these sins in the future?)

*(Ask God to forgive you by devoutly recit-
ing the "Act of Contrition.")*

Dear Lord, natural sleep is a figure of the
sleep of death. Some day shall be my last day
upon earth. Then I shall go to my true and
eternal home of heaven. Make me ready for
that last day on earth and first day in eternity.
My soul waits for the Lord. I trust in his word.

Out of the depths I cry to you, O Lord. Lord, hear my voice. I trust in you, O my God.

Sacred Heart of Jesus, have mercy on my poor soul. Immaculate Heart of Mary, intercede with your Son to bestow his love and grace upon me. As the great woman of faith, O Mary, as the Mother of the Church, keep me always loyal and true in the knowledge and practice of my holy Catholic faith.

Angels of heaven, watch over me this night. My guardian angel, keep my soul holy and pure this night through your intercessory power. St. (name), my patron saint, intercede for me that I may be brought safely home one day.

(Add any other favorite prayers. It is good to spend time in meditation.)

Prayer for Temperance

Dear Jesus, I fear the misuse of your gift of drink. I cannot trust myself. I find it too easy to fool myself and justify my actions. I must work at this problem as though all depended upon me and pray as though all depended upon you, dear Lord. Without you, I can do nothing.

When you hung upon the cross, dear Jesus, you said, "I thirst." You thirsted for my

salvation. May my drink not be to my condemnation and to the unhappiness of others.
Give me strength of will. Give me humility to
seek the help of others and not to avoid
others in my pride who can help me in my
problem. Give me the grace, just for today, to
come to rest, without slavery to drink or a victim of abuse, but living in the knowledge and
love of your grace. Amen.

A Girl's Prayer
Before a Date

Dear God, keep me in your love on this
date. May I return home closer to you because I have found a reflection of your
goodness in my friend. Help me to be an at-
tractive and interesting friend who is considerate of my companion. Grant us the grace to
avoid temptations and be a source to each
other in Christ of greater fulfillment of young
love that is pure and wholesome. Amen.

A Boy's Prayer
Before a Date

Dear God, you are love itself. Help me to
share in your love by the company I shall have

in my friend on this date. I must be mindful that I am to be the protector in your name on this date. I must reflect your goodness, your strength that is wholesome, pure and enjoyable. Help us to avoid deliberate temptations of places and circumstances. If my date is truly a Christian date, I should return home closer to you, dear Lord. May our knowledge and love of one another grow if this be your will. Amen.

Prayer of a Student in School

Dear Lord, you are truth itself. Everything I learn and discover is but a further penetration into you who are the way, the truth and the life. My studies are difficult at times. Because of the fall of our first parents, my mind has been darkened and my will weakened. By your grace and by using the talents you have given me, I must work to the best of my ability to come to a greater understanding of your power and ways in the things of this world which lead to heaven.

Help me, dear Lord, to develop the powers you have placed in my intellect and to willingly share your knowledge with others. Amen.

Prayer of Parents For Their Children

Almighty God, you have called us to the holy state of matrimony and have shared with us your gift of creation. We thank you for making our love fruitful. May we be worthy representatives of you, dear Lord, in forming our children in your knowledge and love.

You have given us children, almighty God, to teach in your ways which will lead to their eternal home of heaven. May our children ever walk in the way of your commandments and live according to the teachings of your holy Catholic Church.

May our example, dear God, be such as to inspire our children to grow into the likeness of your Son, Jesus Christ. May we be firm but kind in discipline. May we stand as one united in authority so as to be consistent. May we never confuse permissiveness with love. May we teach our children respect for your authority in ourselves and in all your representatives upon earth.

May our home be as a Church, for you are present, Lord Jesus Christ, wherever two or three are gathered together in your name. May the praises of God frequently rise from the lips and hearts of our family and may we all one day be united in our eternal home. Amen.

Prayer to Our Lady of Life
(In reparation for abortions)

Lady of life, Mother of the living, I beseech your intercession in reparation for all the abortive murders of unborn babies that take place in our country and in the world. You are the spouse of the Holy Spirit. Intercede then, O Holy Mother of God, that the wisdom of the Holy Spirit may enlighten all men to realize that the destruction of human life at any stage of its development is against the fifth commandment, "You shall not kill."

Mary, when you conceived the child Jesus, the author of life, you became the Mother of life. When the angel Gabriel announced to you, O lady, that you had won God's favor and said, "Listen! You are to conceive and bear a Son, and you must name him Jesus; he will be great and will be called Son of the most high . . .," at that time you went as quickly as you could to a town in the hill country of Judah. You went into Zechariah's house and greeted Elizabeth. The angel Gabriel had said to you, O lady of life, "Know this too: your kinswoman Elizabeth has, in her old age, herself conceived a son, and she whom people called barren is now in her sixth month, for nothing is impossible to God." Now as soon as Elizabeth heard your greeting, O lady of life, the child leapt in Elizabeth's womb and she was filled with the Holy Spirit. She gave a loud cry and said, "Of all women you are the most blessed, and blessed is the fruit of your womb. Why should I be honored with a visit from the Mother of my Lord? For the moment your greeting reached my ears, the child in my womb leapt for joy."

What can we make of this word of God, O lady of life? You have just conceived the Christ Child and immediately go to visit your cousin Elizabeth in her sixth month. Speaking under the inspiration of the Holy Spirit, Elizabeth addresses you, our lady of life, with the title, "Mother of my Lord." The angel spoke of Elizabeth's child in her sixth month as having "conceived a son." Mary, you having conceived in only a matter of days and Elizabeth after six months, but both of you are called mothers and you both bear children whom the word of God calls sons. And yet we have in the world today, men who would destroy human life at almost any stage of human development.

O lady of life, Mother of the word, Mother of all men, intercede with your divine Son, Jesus Christ, and in the unity of the Holy Spirit whose wisdom is ignored by so many and who deprive human souls of the opportunity for rebirth in baptism, grant that all of mankind may recognize the dignity and have that respect for human life from the first moment of its conception. In this way we shall accept God as our Father for we are truly then living as brothers and sisters of Jesus Christ.

Sweet heavenly queen, to your powerful intercession, I wish to join the intercession of St. Joseph and all the angels and saints and in particular that of St. Gerard Majella who has been named the patron and protector of the mother and the unborn child. This saint during life was falsely accused of crime but now he has been raised up by God to intercede for expectant mothers and to protect by his intercession unborn babies from the crimes of men. O blessed lady, queen of all angels and saints, stand before the heavenly throne and bring an end to the crimes of men who are anti-life. Amen.

A Doctor's Prayer

Dear Lord, you are the divine physician. You have called me to mend men's bodies and minds. I can prescribe, but only you, almighty God, can cure and heal. In my vocation, you deliver the care of men's lives into my hands. Help me to make the right decisions in harmony with your divine will. We are growing in the knowledge of medicine but we must use your knowledge justly and responsibly before you and our fellowman. May I form an honest and correct conscience, and respect that of others. May I not fear to witness you, dear Lord, in righteousness before men when despair and problems are apt to distort their judgments and hinder their moral courage. May I always remember, that one day, I must answer before you, almighty God, for the lives you have entrusted to me. In all my decisions and medical actions, almighty God, I desire to be pro-life. Amen.

Prayer to St. Michael
The Archangel

St. Michael the Archangel, defend us in the day of battle; be our safeguard against the wickedness and snares of the devil. May God rebuke him, we humbly pray, and do you, O prince of the heavenly host, by the power of God, cast into hell, Satan and all the other evil spirits, who prowl through the world, seeking the ruin of souls. Amen.

Prayer for Priests (I)

O divine Savior, you are the friend of priests. Send daily into the hearts of all priests the seven gifts of your Holy Spirit that they may become all things to all men both in life and in death.

Give them patience with the little children and the love that you had for them. Make them the chief example of Christ, the teacher, in their parishes. Grant priests compassion on the sick, humility with the poor and courage to withstand the enemies of your holy Church.

Dear Jesus, make priests tireless in teaching your word in faithfulness to the teachings of your Church. Make them patient and kind in the confessional, generous in the administration of holy communion. Let them appear terrible to hell and the powers of evil and to all who side therewith, and let your priests be as messengers of peace to all men of good will.

Withersoever your priests go, may your blessing accompany them. Wheresoever they abide, may your peace enter in. Whomsoever they bless, may he also be blessed by you, O God. Make them apostles. Make them saints. Amen.

Prayer for Priests (II)

Keep them, I pray you, dearest Lord,
Keep them, for they are yours,

Your priests whose lives burn out
   before
Your consecrated shrine.
Keep them, and comfort them in hours
Of loneliness and pain,
When all their life of sacrifice
For souls seems but in vain.
Keep them, and remember, O Lord,
They have no one but you,
Yet they have only human hearts
With human frailty.
Keep them as spotless as the host
That daily they caress,
Their every thought, word, and deed
Deign, dearest Lord, to bless. Amen.

Prayer of Pope Paul VI
To Obtain Faith

Lord, I believe; I wish to believe in thee.

Lord, let my faith be full and unreserved, and let it penetrate my thought, my way of judging divine things and human things.

Lord, let my faith be free; that is, let it have my personal adherence, let it accept the renunciations and duties that this entails and let it express the culminating point of my personality: I believe in thee, Lord.

Lord, let my faith be certain; certain with the appropriate external proofs and with the interior testimony of the Holy Spirit, with the certainty of its reassuring light, its soothing conclusion, its quiet assimilation.

Lord, let my faith be strong, let it not fear the difficulties or the problems of which the experience of our life, eager for light, is full; let it not fear the hostility of those who question it, attack it, reject it, deny it; but let it be strengthened in the intimate proof of thy truth, let it resist the attack of criticism, let it be strengthened in continual affirmation overcoming the dialectic and spiritual difficulties of our temporal existence.

Lord, let my faith be joyful and give peace and gladness to my spirit, and dispose it for prayer with God and conversation with men, so that the inner bliss of its fortunate possession may shine forth in sacred and secular conversation.

Lord, let my faith be industrious and give to charity the reasons of its moral expansion so that there may be true friendship with thee and that in works, in sufferings, in the expectation of the final revelation there may be continual search of thee, a continual testimony to thee, a continuous nourishment of hope in thee.

Lord, let my faith be humbled and not presume to be based on the experience of my thought and of my feeling; but let it surrender to the testimony of the Holy Spirit, and not have any better guarantee than in docility to

tradition and to the authority of the magisterium of holy Church. Amen.

Prayer for a Happy Death

Jesus, Mary and Joseph, I give you my heart
and soul.

Jesus, Mary and Joseph, assist me in my last
agony.

Jesus, Mary and Joseph, let me breathe forth
my spirit in peace with you.

From a sudden and unprovided death, deliver
us, O Lord.

O dear Lord, deliver me from a sudden
and unprovided death. Help me always to live
in your grace, that I may always be ready to
meet you as my maker and my judge at any
moment. Grant me the grace of receiving the
last sacraments, the sacred anointing; your
body and blood, soul and divinity in holy vi-
aticum.

Grant me, O Lord, time for repenting of
any past sins of which I may still be guilty
when my hour comes. Grant that I may die in
the state of grace so that I may be able to live
in your presence forever. I long to see you
face-to-face, even as you are, unworthy
though I be.

I know that I do not deserve everlasting
happiness in heaven. Through no merits of my

own, only through your love and mercy, can I trust in eternal salvation through the merits of Jesus Christ who died on the cross.

Merciful heart of Jesus, by your agony, by your sweat of precious blood, by your scourging at the pillar, shed again on the cross, I ask for salvation for myself, my family, my friends, for everyone near and dear to me. Grant salvation to the whole world.

O Mary, queen and Mother, pray for us now and at the hour of our death. St. Joseph, patron of a happy death, pray for us, that as you died in the arms of Jesus and Mary, we too, may die in their favor and spend eternity in heaven with almighty God, all the angels and saints. Amen.

Prayer for Vocations

O dearest Jesus, Son of the eternal Father and Mary immaculate, grant to our boys and girls, the generosity necessary to follow your call, and the courage required to overcome all obstacles to their vocation.

Give to parents, that faith, love and spirit of sacrifice, which will inspire them to offer their children to God's service, and cause them to rejoice exceedingly, whenever one of their children is called to the religious life.

Let your example, and that of your

blessed Mother and St. Joseph, encourage both children and parents, and let your grace sustain them. Amen.

The Divine Praises

Blessed be God. Blessed be his holy name. Blessed be Jesus Christ, true God and true man. Blessed be the name of Jesus. Blessed be his most Sacred Heart. Blessed be his most precious blood. Blessed be Jesus in the most holy sacrament of the altar. Blessed be the Holy Spirit, the Paraclete. Blessed be the great Mother of God, Mary most holy. Blessed be her holy and immaculate conception. Blessed be her glorious assumption. Blessed be the name of Mary, Virgin and Mother. Blessed be St. Joseph, her most chaste spouse. Blessed be God in his angels and in his saints.

Benediction of the Most Blessed Sacrament

(At the opening of benediction this hymn must be sung.)
Down in adoration falling,
Lo! The sacred host we hail;
Lo! O'er ancient forms departing

Newer rites of grace prevail;
Faith for all defects supplying
Where the feeble senses fail.
To the everlasting Father
And the Son who reigns on high,
With the Spirit blest proceeding
Forth from each eternally,
Be salvation, honor, blessing,
Might, and endless majesty. Amen.

You have given them bread from heaven. (P.T. Alleluia).

Having all sweetness within it.(P.T. Alleluia).

Celebrant: Let us pray: O God, who in this wonderful sacrament left us a memorial of your passion, grant, we implore you, that we may so venerate the sacred mysteries of your body and blood as always to be conscious of the fruit of your redemption. You who live and reign with God the Father in the unity of the Holy Spirit, God, forever and ever. Amen.

Prayer to the Blessed Trinity Before the Blessed Sacrament
(Fatima children)

O most holy Trinity, Father, Son and Holy Spirit, I adore you profoundly. I offer you the most precious body, blood, soul and divinity of Jesus Christ, present in all the tabernacles of the world, in reparation for the outrages, sacrileges and indifferences by which he is offended. By the infinite merits of the Sacred Heart of Jesus and the Immaculate Heart of Mary, I beg the conversion of sinners.

Prayers to the Most Blessed Trinity While in the State of Grace

(The soul that is in the state of sanctifying grace has the three Persons of the one true God, Father, Son and Holy Spirit, really and truly dwelling within it. When one is in grace, his body and soul are as a temple to God living within it. We can pray to the triune God as he lives within us.)

My God, I believe that when I am in your grace, you are living and active within me with all your three Persons. I give you thanks for having created me and keeping me in existence at every second of time. You have loved me with an everlasting love, although I am nothing in myself, and it was your great love, in and through the Sacred Heart of Jesus, that brought me into existence and preserves me this day.

Father, Son and Holy Spirit, keep me when I sleep. Keep me while I go about my daily activities. Keep me from all dangers. May your grace, your divine life, always be within me.

Most holy Trinity, I have found my heaven upon earth. For heaven is where God is, and God is in my soul. I cannot always be in your sacramental presence within your temples made by human hands where you dwell in the tabernacles of our Catholic Church buildings. I *do* consider that a great honor to adore your divine Son, become man, and present under sacramental forms. Also, I cannot always have your divine Son, made man, always sacramentally present within me as he is during those minutes after I have received him in holy communion. And I *privilege* those minutes above *all* upon earth. But, dear God, I can always have your three divine Persons, present really and truly within me when I am in the state of sanctifying grace.

O most holy Trinity, I adore you who are dwelling by your grace within my soul.

O most holy Trinity, who are dwelling by your grace within my soul, make me love you more and more.

O most holy Trinity, who are dwelling by your grace within my soul, sanctify me more and more. Amen.

Aspirations

(The following short prayers, called aspi-

rations, the favorite of which could soon be committed to memory, will be valuable to the devout Catholic in supernaturalizing the entire day. In moments when the mind is uplifted to God, they will prove valuable.)

My God and my all.

Blessed be the name of the Lord!

My God, I give you thanks for what you give, and for what you take away; your will be done.

Teach me, O Lord, to do your will, for you are my God.

O God, be merciful to me, the sinner.

Into your hands, O Lord, I commend my spirit.

O God, come unto my assistance; O Lord, make haste to help me.

Lord, save us, we perish.

Thy will be done!

Lord, I am nothing, but, although nothing, I adore you.

Lord, increase our faith.

My God, I love you.

I believe in you, I hope in you, I love you, I adore you, O blessed Trinity, one God; have mercy on me now and at the hour of my death and save me.

Jesus, Mary and Joseph.

Our Lady of Lourdes *(or under another title approved by ecclesiastical authority),* pray for us.

My Mother, my hope.

O Mary, conceived without sin, pray for us who have recourse to you.

May the Sacred Heart of Jesus be loved in every place.

Heart of Jesus, burning with love for us, set our hearts on fire with love of you.

O Sacred Heart of Jesus, I put my trust in you.

O sacrament most holy, O sacrament divine, all praise and all thanksgiving, be every moment thine.

My Jesus, mercy.

Jesus, Mary, I love you. Save souls.

My Lord and my God. *(Especially at the moment of elevation of the sacred host and chalice at Mass.)*

All for you, most Sacred Heart of Jesus.

Pray for us, O holy Mother of God, that we may be made worthy of the promises of Christ.

Mother of mercy, pray for us.

O Mary, Virgin, Mother of God, pray to Jesus for me.

O Mary, Mother of grace and Mother of mercy, do protect us from our enemy, and receive us at the hour of our death.

Heart of Jesus, burning with love of us, make our hearts to burn with love of you.

Sweet heart of my Jesus, grant that I may love you more and more.

Most Sacred Heart of Jesus, have mercy on us.

Sacred Heart of Jesus, strengthened in your agony by an angel, strengthen us in our agony.

Sacred Heart of Jesus, let me love you and make you loved.

Sorrowful and Immaculate Heart of Mary, pray for us.

Prayer Before
A Parish Council Meeting

Come, Holy Spirit, enlighten our hearts with your wisdom and counsel. Fill us with the desire of the love of God. Help us to keep a perspective that we are to serve, not to rule. Instill in our hearts loyalty to Mother Church, to our pope, our bishop, our pastor. Keep us ever mindful that we are to represent, not simply ourselves or the grievance of some petty group but truly to represent God's people in our entire parish family.

Almighty and eternal God, you search men's hearts. You know the secrets of each one. You are completely open and honest and desire the same with your children in relationship to you and with each other. You came upon earth not to be served, but to serve. Make us realize that our position on this parish council is not to replace the authority of bishop or pastor but to advise and work for the unity of the family of God.

Do not limit our views to our own parish family but give us that wider view of the Church as found in the diocese, nation and the world. But let us not become so global-minded that we fail to see other men's problems but not our own. Help us to build constructively in solving problems and not merely criticize destructively. Let us pray as though all depended upon you, almighty God, and work as though all depended upon us, in the unity of the Holy Spirit, through the love and knowledge of our Lord, Jesus Christ. Amen.

Prayer Before a Parish
School Board Meeting

Come, Holy Spirit, fill us with the light of your knowledge, your wisdom and counsel. Instill in our minds an understanding of the challenges that are ours in religious education. Help us to be practical. Make us realize that the real test of the success of our programs of religious education will be if our young people come to a greater knowledge and love of God in Jesus Christ our Lord and Savior and live their faith in practical day-today living in harmony with the teachings of the holy, catholic and apostolic Church.

Dear Lord, you love the little children. You wanted them to come unto you and did not want anyone to hinder their approach or their love. Let us serve you, Lord Jesus, in the youth of our parish that we may direct, say and do only that which will work for the unity of all the people of this parish family unto the education and formation of young people in Christ Jesus. May we be instrumental also in bringing people of all ages and all levels of education to closer union with you, Lord Jesus.

May we be truly aware of the religion programs, the content, the attitudes, and goals set forth in our school. May we listen to the parents of the children of our school since parents are the first educators. May we implement the teachings of our holy father, the pope and the bishops and in union with them, be instruments of the voice of Christ to the lambs of the flock of our parish. May we all meet one day together in our true home which is heaven. Amen.

Prayer to Thank God for Favors

Dear God, you have said to us in your Son, Jesus Christ, "Ask and you shall receive."

I thank you for answering my poor prayers. I have not deserved to be heard and yet, you always hear me and favor me with your blessings. I have knocked and you have opened the door of your heart. Thank you, dear God.

So often, dear Lord, have I sinned against you that I am not worthy to be called your child. And yet, you continue to answer my prayers. Forgive me, and bestow upon me the best of your gifts that will work for my salvation. Help me, almighty and loving God, not to use or abuse your created gifts, the possessions you have given me, the opportunities offered, in such a way that these be for my own condemnation. Rather, Lord, may every good gift coming from you, the Father above, be unto your honor and glory, my salvation and that of the whole world, through Jesus Christ, your only Son our Lord, who lives and reigns in the unity of the Holy Spirit, world without end. Amen.

Prayer to Find Work

Lord, I am out of work. I know not where to turn. I wish to use these hands, this mind, to support myself and others. I fear, dear Lord. You have said, "Ask and you shall receive. . . . Knock and it shall be opened unto you."

Please, I beg you for the opportunity to serve you in some area of life that will assist in my support and that of others.

I do not ask for work that flatters my pride. I am willing to do your will in humble ways, if only you will hear me, O Lord. I promise to work conscientiously and share your blessings with others, if only, dear Lord, you will answer me. I place my trust in you, dear Lord. Amen.

Prayer to Do
The Will of God

Almighty and eternal God, ruler of the universe, ever present around, beneath, above and within me, behold, I come to do your will, O God. I know not what to do. My mind is darkened. My will is weak. I am weary and lonely and I ask again, "Lord, what will you have me to do?"

I find the circumstances of my life hard, at times, O God. I do not understand why things happen the way they do. Then, I remember your divine Son, Jesus Christ, as his soul was sorrowful unto death. In the garden he sweat his precious blood in agony and found the divine will of his heavenly Father difficult. And he prayed — *Lord Jesus, you prayed!* — "Not my will, but yours be done."

On the cross, O Jesus, you prayed, asking why your heavenly Father had forsaken you. You knew that he had not, but in your human nature you felt desolation. You became a man in all things but sin — and so you knew what it was to be forsaken. You prayed: "Into your hands, I commend my spirit."

Not understanding perfectly, not knowing the reasons why for many things, I come before you, almighty God, to be strengthened, to accept your will as Jesus Christ, my Lord and Savior, accepted the will of his heavenly Father. I am all yours, almighty God, and all that I have is yours. Your kingdom come. Your will be done. Amen.

Prayer of Children For Their Parents

Divine Savior, I ask that you bless my mother and father. I thank you for giving me my particular parents. Of all the parents in the world you could have used to bring me into the world, you chose the love of my parents and the love you have for them and for me. Before you created my parents, or me, you said to us, "I have loved you with an everlasting love." You first loved us. Then you made us in your image and likeness, almighty God.

I thank you, dear God, for using my

parents as your instruments in bestowing
upon me the holy Catholic faith. I want my
parents to go to heaven. I desire to be in heaven
with them someday. Help me not to disappoint
you or them, dear Lord.

My parents have sacrificed much for me,
O Lord. I have not showed them appreciation
and sufficient love. Yet, like you, in so many
ways, they continue to forgive me and to love
me. Help me, dear Lord, to improve, to grow
in love and appreciation for my parents, by
the kind of life I lead that will be pleasing to
you and to them, through Jesus Christ, my
Lord and Savior. Amen.

Prayer on Pay Day

Lord, today I receive from your abundance.
You gave me this job and it is through
your love and mercy that I receive this pay. I
am to use this money not for selfish purposes
but for your honor and glory. I must manifest
your love in the way I use this money for the
welfare of others.

Give me wisdom, dear Lord, to spend this
money prudently. I must not use it for mere
worldly purposes or permissively share it with
children so that they do not appreciate your
blessings. And yet, I must be generous in
using it to provide for my own needs and that

of others. May I not neglect the poor. May I not neglect charitable causes and the support of your holy Church. May I become ever more conscious that this pay I receive, must be earned so that in justice I return the work for the pay that your mercy provides.

Help me, dear Lord, to be diligent to use the talents you gave me unto increase. And may I use the increase for the increase of your love. When my pay is great, I will thank you for your abundance; and share your blessings. When my pay is small, I shall thank you still and strive by diligence to improve my lot and that of others. I am grateful, dear Lord, for whatever you give me and wish to return love to you for the love you have shown me. Amen.

(TRADITIONAL PRAYERS)

Our Father

Our Father, who art in heaven, hallowed be thy name; thy kingdom come, thy will be done on earth as it is in heaven. Give us this day our daily bread; and forgive us our trespasses as we forgive those who trespass against us; and lead us not into temptation but deliver us from evil. Amen.

Hail Mary

Hail Mary, full of grace; the Lord is with thee; blessed art thou among women, and blessed is the fruit of thy womb, Jesus.

Holy Mary, Mother of God, pray for us sinners, now and at the hour of our death. Amen.

An Act of Contrition

O my God! I am heartily sorry for having offended thee, and I detest all my sins, because I dread the loss of heaven and the pains of hell, but most of all because they offend thee, my God, who are all-good and deserving of all my love. I firmly resolve with the help of thy grace, to confess my sins, to do penance, and to amend my life. Amen.

The Apostles' Creed

I believe in God, the Father almighty, creator of heaven and earth; and in Jesus Christ, his only Son, our Lord; who was conceived by the Holy Spirit, born of the Virgin Mary, suffered under Pontius Pilate, was crucified, died, and was buried; he descended into hell, the third day he arose from the dead; he as-

cended into heaven, sitteth at the right hand
of God, the Father almighty; from thence he
shall come to judge the living and the dead. I
believe in the Holy Spirit, the holy Catholic
Church, the communion of saints, the forgiveness of sins, the resurrection of the body, and
life everlasting. Amen.

An Act of Faith

O my God! I firmly believe that thou art
one God in three divine Persons, Father, Son
and Holy Spirit. I believe that thy divine Son
became man, and died for our sins, and that
he will come to judge the living and the dead.
I believe these and all the truths which the
holy Catholic Church teaches, because thou
hast revealed them, who canst neither deceive
nor be deceived.

An Act of Hope

O my God! Relying upon thy infinite
goodness and promises, I hope to obtain pardon for my sins, the help of thy grace, and life
everlasting, through the merits of Jesus Christ,
my Lord and Redeemer.

An Act of Love

O my God! I love you above all things with my whole heart and soul, because you are all-good and worthy of all love. I love my neighbor as myself for the love of you. I forgive all who have injured me, and ask pardon of all whom I have injured.

Glory Be

Glory be to the Father, and to the Son, and to the Holy Spirit.

As it was in the beginning, is now, and ever shall be, world without end. Amen.

The Blessing Before Meals

Bless us, O Lord, and these thy gifts, which we are about to receive from thy bounty, through Christ our Lord. Amen.

Grace After Meals

We give thee thanks, almighty God, for all thy benefits, which we have received from thy bounty, through Christ our Lord.

Morning Offering

O Jesus, through the Immaculate Heart of Mary, I offer you my prayers, works, joys and sufferings of this day in union with the holy sacrifice of the Mass throughout the world. I offer them for all the intentions of your Sacred Heart: the salvation of souls, reparation for sin, the reunion of all Christians; I offer them for the intentions of our bishops and of all members of the apostleship of prayer, and in particular for those recommended by our holy father this month.

The Angelus

V. The angel of the Lord declared unto Mary.

R. And she conceived of the Holy Spirit. Hail Mary, etc.

V. Behold the handmaid of the Lord.

R. Be it done unto me according to thy word. Hail Mary, etc.

V. And the Word was made flesh.

R. And dwelt among us. Hail Mary, etc.

V. Pray for us, O holy Mother of God.

R. That we may be made worthy of the promises of Christ.

Let us pray:

Pour forth, we beseech thee, O Lord, thy

grace into our hearts, that we to whom the incarnation of Christ, thy Son, was made known by the message of an angel, may by his passion and cross be brought to the glory of his resurrection, through the same Christ our Lord. Amen.

Prayer to the Holy Spirit

Come, Holy Spirit, fill the hearts of thy faithful and enkindle in them the fire of thy love.

V. Send forth thy Spirit and they shall be created.

R. And thou shall renew the face of the earth.

Let us pray:

O God, who didst instruct the hearts of the faithful by the light of the Holy Spirit, grant us in the same Spirit to be truly wise, and ever to rejoice in his consolation. Through Christ our Lord. Amen.

Mysteries of the Rosary

(Meditate on these mysteries while reciting the Hail Marys.)

Joyful Mysteries:

1. The Annunciation — The angel tells Mary she is to be the Mother of the Savior.

2. The Visitation — Mary in charity goes to visit her cousin Elizabeth.
3. The Nativity — Jesus is born to Mary.
4. The Presentation of the Child Jesus in the Temple — Mary and Joseph take the child to the temple to fulfill the law.
5. The Finding of the Child Jesus in the Temple — After three days.

Sorrowful Mysteries:
1. The Agony in the Garden — Our sins weigh upon Jesus.
2. The Scourging at the Pillar — Jesus is scourged for our sins.
3. The Crowning with Thorns — Thorns pierce our Lord's head.
4. Jesus Carries the Cross — He carries it to Calvary for us.
5. The Crucifixion — For three hours Jesus suffers intensely on the cross.

Glorious Mysteries:
1. Resurrection — Jesus rises from the dead.
2. The Ascension — After forty days Jesus ascends bodily to heaven.
3. The Descent of the Holy Spirit — In the form of tongues of fire.
4. The Assumption — Mary's body is taken into heaven.
5. The Crowning of the Blessed Virgin — Mary is queen of heaven and earth.

Stations of the Cross

(The stations can be offered any time, simply by pausing at each station and reflecting briefly on any event of our Lord's passion and death.)

Stations:

First: Jesus is condemned to death.
    It was my sins that condemned you to death. I am sorry. Save me from eternal death.

Second: Jesus carries the cross.
    The cross of Jesus is really my sins and those of others. O Jesus, by my future life, may I lessen its weight.

Third: Jesus falls the first time.
    The weight of my sins crushes you to the ground. It reminds me of my first mortal sin. Give me the grace never more to offend you, dear Jesus.

Fourth: Jesus meets his blessed Mother.
    Sorrowful and Immaculate Heart of Mary, my sins offended you too. Jesus suffers to see your sorrowful heart. Jesus, Mary, I am sorry for sin.

Fifth: Simon helps Jesus carry the cross.
    I want to help you carry the cross also. I can, by a better Christian life.

I can, by accepting the crosses you permit in my life.

Sixth: Veronica wipes the face of Jesus.

Jesus, you left the imprint of your sacred face on Veronica's cloth. Place upon my soul your sacred image. Place my image in your Sacred Heart.

Seventh: Jesus falls the second time.

It reminds me of my second fall into mortal sin. Even my venial sins are thorns in your Sacred Heart. By your grace, may I never fall into sin again.

Eighth: Jesus speaks to the women of Jerusalem.

Your thoughts, O Jesus, are not of self, but of your Father and the millions of souls you must save. May I too show such loving concern.

Ninth: Jesus falls the third time.

The sins of the whole world, including mine, bend you to the ground again, Jesus. You get up, so I can rise from sin. Draw all the world to yourself.

Tenth: Jesus is stripped of his garments.

Not even clothes will they permit Jesus to wear to his death as he detaches himself from everything to attach us to his heart and to his Father.

Eleventh: Jesus is nailed to the cross.

"With Jesus I am nailed to the cross," and so I shall henceforth be by a life of love, faith, hope, penance. The crown, the thorns, spikes I feel.

Twelfth: Jesus dies on the cross.

For three hours you thirst and suffer immeasurably for souls and the glory of our Father. You die so that I might live. "For me to live is Christ."

Thirteenth: Jesus is taken down from the Cross.

The sorrowful Mother now truly has her heart pierced with a sword. Jesus has saved sinners. Mother, intercede to apply his saving graces.

Fourteenth: Jesus is laid in the tomb.

Even your tomb is borrowed. But you will not need it long, for you are life itself. By your passion, death, resurrection and ascension, heaven awaits us.

(It is good to conclude the stations of the cross with reflection on the resurrection. Add prayers for our holy father, the pope, e.g., Our Father, Hail Mary, Glory be. . . .)

Litany of the
Sacred Heart of Jesus

Lord, have mercy on us.
Christ, have mercy on us.
Lord, have mercy on us. Christ, hear us.
Christ, graciously hear us.
God the Father of heaven, *have mercy on us.*
God the Son, Redeemer of the world, **(After each invocation, respond with,** *"Have mercy on us."***)**
God the Holy Spirit,
Holy Trinity, one God,
Heart of Jesus, Son of the eternal Father,
Heart of Jesus, formed by the Holy Spirit in the womb of the Virgin Mother,
Heart of Jesus, united substantially with the word of God,
Heart of Jesus of infinite majesty,
Heart of Jesus, holy temple of God,
Heart of Jesus, tabernacle of the most high,
Heart of Jesus, house of God and gate of heaven,
Heart of Jesus, glowing furnace of charity,
Heart of Jesus, vessel of justice and love,
Heart of Jesus, full of goodness and love,
Heart of Jesus, abyss of all virtues,
Heart of Jesus, most worthy of all praise,
Heart of Jesus, king and center of all hearts,
Heart of Jesus, in whom are all the treasures of wisdom and knowledge,

Heart of Jesus, in whom dwells all the fullness of divinity,

Heart of Jesus, in whom the Father is well pleased,

Heart of Jesus, in whose fullness we have all received,

Heart of Jesus, desire of the eternal hills,

Heart of Jesus, patient and rich in mercy,

Heart of Jesus, rich to all who invoke you,

Heart of Jesus, fount of life and holiness,

Heart of Jesus, propitiation for our sins,

Heart of Jesus, loaded down with opprobrium,

Heart of Jesus, bruised for our offenses,

Heart of Jesus, made obedient unto death,

Heart of Jesus, pierced with a lance,

Heart of Jesus, source of all consolation,

Heart of Jesus, our life and resurrection,

Heart of Jesus, our peace and reconciliation,

Heart of Jesus, victim for our sins,

Heart of Jesus, salvation of those who hope in you,

Heart of Jesus, hope of those who die in you,

Heart of Jesus, delight of all saints,

Lamb of God, who takes away the sins of the world, *spare us, O Lord.*

Lamb of God, who takes away the sins of the world, *graciously hear us, O Lord.*

Lamb of God, who takes away the sins of the world, *have mercy on us.*

V. Jesus, meek and humble of heart.

R. Make our hearts like unto yours.

Let us pray:

Almighty and everlasting God, graciously regard the heart of your well-beloved Son and the acts of praise and satisfaction which he renders you on behalf of us sinners; and through your merit, grant pardon to us who implore your mercy, in the name of your Son Jesus Christ, who lives and reigns with you in the unity of the Holy Spirit, God, world without end. Amen.

Litany of the Blessed Virgin

Lord, have mercy on us.
Christ, have mercy on us.
Lord, have mercy on us.
Christ, hear us.
Christ, graciously hear us.
God, the Father of heaven, *have mercy on us.*
God, the Son, Redeemer of the world, *have mercy on us.*
God, the Holy Spirit, *have mercy on us.*
Holy Trinity, one God, *have mercy on us.*
Holy Mary, *pray for us.*
Holy Mother of God, **(After each invocation, respond with,** *"Pray for us."***)**
Holy Virgin of virgins,
Mother of Christ,

Mother of divine grace,
Mother most pure,
Mother most chaste,
Mother inviolate,
Mother undefiled,
Mother most amiable,
Mother most admirable,
Mother of good counsel,
Mother of our Creator,
Mother of our Savior,
Virgin most prudent,
Virgin most venerable,
Virgin most renowned,
Virgin most powerful,
Virgin most merciful,
Virgin most faithful,
Mirror of justice,
Seat of wisdom,
Cause of our joy,
Spiritual vessel,
Vessel of honor,
Vessel of singular devotion,
Mystical rose,
Tower of David,
Tower of ivory,
House of gold,
Ark of the covenant,
Gate of heaven,
Morning star,
Health of the sick,
Refuge of sinners,

Comforter of the afflicted,

Help of Christians,

Queen of angels,

Queen of patriarchs,

Queen of prophets,

Queen of apostles,

Queen of martyrs,

Queen of confessors,

Queen of virgins,

Queen of all saints,

Queen conceived without original sin,

Queen assumed into heaven,

Queen of the most holy rosary,

Queen of peace,

Lamb of God, who takes away the sins of the world, *spare us, O Lord.*

Lamb of God, who takes away the sins of the world, *graciously hear us, O Lord.*

Lamb of God, who takes away the sins of the world, *have mercy on us.*

V. Pray for us, O Holy Mother of God.

R. That we may be made worthy of the promises of Christ.

Let us pray:

Grant, we beseech you, O Lord God, that we, your servants, may enjoy perpetual health of soul and body; and by the glorious intercession of blessed Mary, ever Virgin, may we be delivered from our present sorrows and rejoice in eternal happiness. Through Christ, our Lord. Amen.

Litany of Mary, Mother of the Church
(From Chapter 8, Dogmatic Constitution on the Church, Vatican II)

Holy God, wishing in your supreme goodness and wisdom to effect the redemption of the world, *have mercy on us.*

God the Father, who sent your Son, born of a woman, *have mercy on us.*

Holy God, wishing that we might receive the adoption of sons, *have mercy on us.*

God the Son, who for us men, and for our salvation, came down from heaven, *have mercy on us.*

God the Son, incarnate by the Holy Spirit from the Virgin Mary, *have mercy on us.*

Glorious and perpetual Virgin Mary, *pray for us.*

Mother of God and our Lord Jesus Christ, **(After each invocation, respond with, "Pray for us.")**

O maiden, at the message of the angel, you received the word of God in your heart and body,

O Mother, redeemed in an especially sublime manner by the merits of your Son,

O Mother, united to the Redeemer by a close and indissoluble tie,

O woman of faith, endowed with the supreme office and dignity of being the Mother of the Son of God,

O maiden, the favorite daughter of the Father,

O maiden, the temple of the Holy Spirit,

O maiden, offspring of Adam and one with all human beings in their need for salvation,

Mary, Mother of the members of Christ the head,

Mary, preeminent and altogether singular member of the Church,

Mary, the Church's model and excellent exemplar in faith and charity,

Mary, Mother of the faithful,

Mary, who occupies a place in the Church, highest after Christ and yet very close to us,

Mary, prophetically foreshadowed in that victory over the serpent promised our first parents,

Holy Virgin, who conceived and bore a Son, whose name was called Emmanuel,

Mary, standing out among the poor and humble of the Lord who confidently await and receive salvation from him,

Mary, from whom the Son of God took a human nature that he might free man from sin,

Mary, who gave to the world that very life which renews all things,

Mother of God, entirely holy and free from all stain of sin,

Mary, fashioned by the Holy Spirit into a kind of new substance and new creature,

Mary, adorned from the first instant of your conception with the splendors of an entirely unique holiness,

Virgin of Nazareth, on God's command, greeted by an angel messenger as "full of grace,"

Mary, a daughter of Adam, Mother of Jesus,

Mary, embracing God's saving will with a full heart and impeded by no sin,

Mary, devoted totally as a handmaid of the Lord to the Person and work of your Son,

Mary, subordinated to Jesus and along with him, by the grace of almighty God, you served the mystery of redemption,

Mary, used by God while cooperating in the work of human salvation through free faith and obedience,

Mary, what the virgin Eve bound through her unbelief, you loosened by your faith,

Mary, greeted by Elizabeth as blessed because of your belief in the promise of salvation,

Queen Mother, your Son, our Lord Jesus, did not diminish your virginal integrity but sanctified it,

Mary, of whom Simeon foretold a sword would pierce your Mother's soul, that out of many hearts thoughts might be revealed,

Mary, who kept all things of Jesus to be pondered over in your heart,

Queen Mother, moved by pity at the marriage

feast of Cana, and whose intercession brought about the beginning of miracles of Jesus, the Messiah,

Mary, who in the course of your Son's preaching received his praise,

Mary, declared blessed because you faithfully heard and kept the word of God,

Mary, who on your pilgrimage of faith, united yourself with a maternal heart to your Son's sacrifice on the cross,

Mary, who consented to the immolation of your Son as victim which you yourself had brought forth,

Mary, Jesus' dying on the cross gave you as a Mother to his disciple when he said: "Woman, behold thy son,"

Mary, Mother of Jesus, seen with the apostles before the day of Pentecost continuing in prayer,

Queen Mother, prayerfully imploring the gift of the Spirit, who had already overshadowed you in the annunciation,

Mary, whose duty toward men does not obscure or diminish the mediation of Christ but shows its power,

O blessed Virgin, eternally predestined, in conjunction with the incarnation of the divine word, to be the Mother of God,

Mary, who presented Jesus to the Father in the temple and was united with him in suffering on the cross,

Mary, who cooperated by your obedience, faith, hope and burning charity in the Savior's work of restoring supernatural life to souls,

Mary, a Mother to us in the order of grace,

Mary, whose maternity will last without interruption until the eternal fulfillment of all the elect,

Queen Mother, whose manifold acts of intercessation continue to win for us gifts of eternal salvation,

Mary, invoked by the Church under the titles which neither add nor take away from Christ the one mediator,

Mary, model of the Church in the matter of faith, charity and perfect union with Christ,

Mary, eminent and singular exemplar of both virginity and motherhood,

Mary, believing and obeying, you brought forth on earth the Father's Son, by being overshadowed by the Holy Spirit,

Mary, becoming a mother by accepting God's word in faith,

Mary, by your preaching and by baptism you bring forth to a new and immortal life, children who are conceived by the Holy Spirit and born of God,

Mary, in whom the Church has already reached that perfection without spot or wrinkle,

Mary, who shines forth to the whole community of the elect as a model of the virtues,

Mary, profoundly figuring in the history of salvation, you unite and mirror within yourself the central truths of the faith,

Mary, who summons the faithful to your Son and his sacrifice and to love for the Father,

Mary, after your Son, exalted by divine grace above all angels and men,

Mary, from most ancient times, venerated under the title of "God-bearer,"

Mary, whom all generations shall call blessed, because he who is mighty has done great things for you,

Mary, to whom devotions cause your Son to be rightly known, loved and glorified and all his commands observed,

Mary, whose offices and privileges are always related to Christ, the source of all truth, sanctity and piety,

Mary, image and first flowering of the Church,

Mary, shining forth on earth as a sign of sure hope and solace for the pilgrim people of God,

Let us pray:

We, the body of the faithful, pour forth persevering prayer to the Mother of God and Mother of men. Mary, you aided the beginnings of the Church by your prayers; now, exalted in heaven above all the saints and angels, intercede with your Son in the fellowship of all the saints. Continue your prayers until all the peoples of the human family, whether they are honored with the name of Christian or whether they still do not know their Savior, are happily gathered together in peace and harmony into the one people of God, for the glory of the most holy and undivided Trinity. Amen.

Litany of the Saints

Lord, have mercy on us. *Lord, have mercy on us.*
Christ, have mercy on us. *Christ, have mercy on us.*
Lord, have mercy on us. *Lord, have mercy on us.*
Holy Mary, Mother of God, *pray for us.*
St. Michael, **(After each invocation, respond with,** *"Pray for us."***)**
Holy angels of God,
St. Joseph,
St. John the Baptist,
St. Peter and St. Paul,
St. Andrew,
St. John,
St. Mary Magdalene,
St. Stephen,
St. Ignatius,

St. Lawrence,

St. Perpetua and St. Felicity,

St. Agnes,

St. Gregory,

St. Augustine,

St. Athanasius,

St. Basil,

St. Martin,

St. Benedict,

St. Francis and St. Dominic,

St. Francis Xavier,

St. John Vianney,

St. Catherine,

St. Theresa,

All you saints of God,

Lord, be merciful. *Lord, save us.*

From all harm, **(After each invocation, respond with,** *"Lord, save us.")*

From every sin,

From all temptations,

From everlasting death,

By your coming among us,

By your death and rising to new life,

By your gift of the Holy Spirit,

Be merciful to us sinners. *Lord, hear our prayer.*

Guide and protect your holy Church. *Lord, hear our prayer.*

Keep our pope and all the clergy in faithful service to your Church. *Lord, hear our prayer.*

Bring all people together in trust and peace.
Lord, hear our prayer.
Strengthen us in your service. *Lord, hear our prayer.*

Let us pray:

From you, Lord, comes holiness in our desires, right thinking in our plans, and justice in our actions. Grant your children that peace which the world cannot give; then our hearts will be devoted to your laws, we shall be delivered from the terrors of war, and under your protection we shall be able to live in tranquillity. Amen.

Hail Holy Queen

Hail, holy queen, Mother of mercy, hail, our life, our sweetness and our hope! To you do we cry, poor banished children of Eve! To you do we send up our sighs, mourning and weeping in this vale of tears. Turn then, most gracious advocate, your eyes of mercy toward us; and after this our exile, show us the blessed fruit of your womb, Jesus. O clement, O loving, O sweet Virgin Mary!

V. Pray for us, O holy Mother of God.

R. That we may be made worthy of the promises of Christ.

Let us pray:

O God, our refuge and strength, look graciously upon your people crying to you; and through the intercession of the glorious and immaculate Virgin Mary, Mother of God, of blessed Joseph her spouse, of thy holy apostles Peter and Paul, and of all the saints, in your mercy and goodness hear our prayers for the conversion of sinners and for the freedom and exaltation of holy Mother Church; through the same Christ our Lord. Amen.

Prayer of Catechists
To the Holy Spirit

O Holy Spirit, God of love, you have chosen me as a vessel to communicate to youth the knowledge and love of the entire blessed Trinity, in, with and through Jesus Christ, the Son of God, Savior. I feel so unworthy. I am not qualified. You know that, but dear God, who is qualified? I have not chosen you, dear Lord; you have chosen me.

You have said in sacred scripture through your great apostle, St. Paul, "The foolish things of the world has God chosen to put to shame the 'wise,' and the weak things of the world has God chosen to put to shame the strong." I am not influential among men by worldly standards. I am weak. And if I remain loyal to Mother Church and the authentic teachings which the one, holy, catholic and apostolic Church voices in and for the Person of Jesus Christ, I will surely be considered foolish and even ridiculed by some.

Dear God, I have come to this task, not to do my will, but yours. I am to teach about you; not about myself. I am to be loyal to the Church's official teachings and not echo the opinions of men. Christ must increase. I must decrease. I am to draw young people to you, Jesus, not to myself. Insofar as they are attracted to me, O Lord, may it be only because they see in me a reflection of your own truth, beauty and goodness.

I am teaching for you, Jesus; not for my parish priest or bishop or anyone else as mere men. They represent you, and, so must I, however limited. I do not look for gratitude except in the joy that souls are coming to your knowledge and love. I know that whatever reward you may have for me, dear God, will essentially be realized in the next life. That is sufficient.

Help me, Holy Spirit, to know and love the true teachings of Christ and so effectively to communicate the "Good News" for the education and formation of youth. I am a helper of parents and of my pastor, and bishop. Give me strength, patience, when I am tried and tired. Help me to promote a spirit of unity, of loyalty, among my fellow catechists and the entire parish. If I am to be an effective instrument of you, my Jesus, I must suffer. *That* was and is still your way. O Holy Spirit, God of love, of myself I can do nothing, but with your assistance, I can do all things, in Christ Jesus, my Lord and the chief teacher of men. Amen.

Prayer for the Holy Father, the Pope

O invisible head of the Church, Jesus Christ, give strength to your visible head upon earth, our holy father, the pope. Of all men upon the face of the earth, you have laid the heaviest burden upon our pope. You have made our pope the servant of servants. You have willed that in bringing men to you, dear Lord, the pope should have to drink the cup of suffering and lay his head upon a crown of thorns. And you have willed that after he has suffered, he should confirm his brothers and sisters in the true Catholic faith.

The world would have our pope, the vicar of Jesus Christ upon earth, speak for and of the world, rather than for you, O God. The world cries that the pope should change your teachings, but you will not permit that. You have said that unless one takes up his cross and follows you, he is not worthy of you. Already, as you first hung on the cross, men cried, "If you are the Son of God, come down from the cross. . . . Let him come down from the cross, *and we will believe in him.*" Isn't that something, dear Lord? They will believe in you if you separate yourself from the cross. And so men say of your pope today, "If he will take the cross out of Christianity, they will believe. Then they will find the Church credible." But God, then the Catholic Church would no longer be the mystical body of Christ, the true Church. You will never permit that. You have promised your Church, "I am with you all days even to the end of the world." To be worthy of you, we must take up the cross daily.

O Holy Spirit, spirit of truth, keep your Church in the truth. We thank you for that, as we know you *will.* But lighten the burden of the pope who must carry that heavy cross of yours today. Unite bishops and priests and the millions of the faithful solidly behind your vicar on earth, that we may live in peace and unity and be drawn to heaven as one. Amen.

Prayer for One's Bishop

Almighty God, may my bishop stand firm and shepherd your flock by your strength, O Lord, in the majesty of your name. May my bishop so guide this diocese that all the priests of the Church will be clothed with justice and truth so as to lead all your people in Jesus' name to eternal salvation.

Make my bishop a strong and fearless leader, dear God, in union with the college of bishops throughout the world and in unity with that chief shepherd on earth, our holy father, the pope. Give them the courage to take a stand, dear Lord. If our bishops do not direct us firmly and clearly with the word of God, we become a flock without a shepherd. Give me, dear Lord, the courage to support my bishop by word and action and to create a spirit of unity among fellow parishioners and among all in this diocese, so that my bishop will know that we welcome the truth, that we will accept obedience, that we will support him when he imitates Christ Jesus in fearless leadership even unto death.

Dear God, my bishop is your chief representative in this diocese. He has the fullness of the priesthood of Jesus Christ, the high priest. Yet, my bishop is only human. He has human feelings and disappointments. Give him strength and give your people strength to stand as one with our bishop in the unity of the Holy Spirit, through Jesus Christ our Lord. Amen.

The Magnificat

(This is Mary's great prayer, from Luke 1:46-55, which the Christian soul should pray in union with her.)

My soul proclaims the greatness of the Lord
and my spirit exults in God my Savior;
because he has looked upon his lowly handmaid.

Yes, from this day forward all generations will call me blessed,
for the almighty has done great things for me.

Holy is his name,
and his mercy reaches from age to age for those who fear him.

He has shown the power of his arm,
he has routed the proud of heart.

He has pulled down princes from their thrones and exalted the lowly.

The hungry he has filled with good things, the rich sent empty away.

He has come to the help of Israel his servant, mindful of his mercy
—according to the promise he made to our ancestors—
of his mercy to Abraham and to his descendants forever. Amen.

Prayer for a Conversion
To the Faith

I do believe, Lord; help my unbelief. My own faith needs strengthening. My love needs rekindling. Yet, I beg from you, Lord Jesus, the grace of conversion to the fullness of true faith for (name), whom I love in this life and desire to love in eternity.

St. Thomas, apostle of Christ, by your intercession, obtain from Jesus in the unity of the Holy Spirit, the gift of conversion for the person for whom I pray. Help him (her) make with you, your profession of faith when you beheld the risen Savior, "My Lord and my God."

May my loved one some day kneel together with me before your altar, Lord, and in faith and in the power of the Holy Spirit, look upon the elevated host being offered to the Father and whisper the prayer of Thomas, "My Lord and my God."

May we together, through your will and intention, one day soon receive the Lord's body, blood, soul and divinity in your holy Catholic Church. May we together approach the sacrament of reconciliation. May we together recite the creed of your holy Catholic Church.

Lord, the gift of faith is your free gift to men. Make me an instrument in your hands to

win the gift of faith by my prayers, good works
and example for (name). Amen.

Prayer for Social
Justice Among Men

Heavenly Father, everyone — regardless
of race, creed or culture — is my brother, my
sister, in and through your Son, Jesus Christ.
The injustice I see among men, and at times
have been guilty of myself, is our failure to appreciate our brotherhood because, dear God,
we have failed to recognize your common Fa-
therhood. You make your sun to shine upon
all men. You have given life to us all and made
us all in your own image and likeness. If you
love us all as your children, we must love and
serve one another as brothers and sisters.

You have called us all, dear God, to the
same holiness, to the same heaven. We are on
but a pilgrimage upon this earth. For eternity
we are destined to share the same true home
of everlasting life together as one. We must
journey to our eternal home together as one
family of God upon this planet earth.

Grant peace and security, even now, to
the poor and the despised, the underpriv-
ileged, the exceptional, those suffering from
the ravages of war and natural disasters of
earth. Have pity on them all, dear Lord, and

help me to realize the equality of men in their rights of life, freedom, happiness in this world and in the next. May I do my part, cooperating with your holy will, to serve you in my fellowmen, dear Jesus.

May I ever be mindful of that vision you have given us of the last judgment: "All the nations will be assembled before him and he will separate men one from another as the shepherd separates sheep from goats. He will place the sheep on his right hand and the goats on his left. Then the king will say to those on his right hand, 'Come, you whom my Father has blessed, take for your heritage the kingdom prepared for you since the foundation of the world. For I was hungry and you gave me food; I was thirsty and you gave me drink; I was a stranger and you made me welcome; naked and you clothed me; sick and you visited me; in prison and you came to see me.' Then the virtuous will say to him in reply, 'Lord, when did we see you hungry and feed you; or thirsty and give you drink? When did we see you a stranger and make you welcome; naked and clothe you; sick or in prison and go to see you?' And the king will answer, 'I tell you solemnly, insofar as you did this to one of the least of these brothers of mine, you did it to me.' Next he will say to those on his left hand, 'Go away from me, with your curse upon you, to the eternal fire prepared for the devil and his angels. . . . I tell you solemnly, insofar as you neglected to do this to one of the least of these, you neglected to do it to me.' And they will go away to eternal punishment, and the virtuous to eternal life."

Dear God, my practice of social justice among men will lead me to heaven.

Prayer for Christian Unity

Lord Jesus, you who prayed "that all may be one," I pray for full unity among all who profess you to be Lord and Savior. Bring together into one fold, under one shepherd, Christians of both East and West. Let your Mother Mary, our lady of the atonement, intercede on our behalf that all Christians may once again eat your body and drink your precious blood at one table and adore the blessed Trinity before one altar.

Dear God, we have all sinned. In some way we are all responsible for Christian disunity in the world today. If each one of us would believe in your Son, Jesus Christ, and live his gospel to the full, there would be no problem to embracing each other as one in our Lord, Jesus Christ.

Open our minds, O Holy Spirit, spirit of unity, and give us that change of heart, that humility that can bridge the gaps that separate us and surmount the barriers that divide us. Each one must be true to his conscience. No one should compromise the truth, and you, Lord Jesus, are the truth.

Make me more Christ-like, dear Lord, so that by my prayers, good works, my very life, I may be a help, not a hindrance, to full unity among all who invoke the name of Jesus. Amen.

Prayer to Contend With Restlessness
(Based on Admonition of Pope Paul VI)

Lord, Jesus Christ, like so many men today, I feel restless at times. Social conditions leave men today divided and dissatisfied; I am no exception. Dear Lord, I turn to your Church and I know that you, Lord Jesus, are the answer. I hear your Church, your mystical body, saying to me:

"Are you hungry? Christ is the bread of life. Are you thirsty? Christ is the source of living waters. Do you need to see and understand? Christ is the light of the world. Do you desire justice and liberty? Christ is the liberator from the shackles of riches and pride. Are you in need of love? Christ is the supreme giver of love — God is love."

Prayer for the Conversion Of Communists and Freedom of All Peoples

Mary, Mother of God and Mother of the Church, through your Immaculate Heart, I implore our heavenly Father for the freedom and conversion of all peoples living under atheistic governments. Many peoples have lost their freedom of religion under godless communism. Many have been enslaved and continue to live in poverty and even away from their families. Many are not able to worship you, almighty God, according to their conscience. Many have been deprived of the sacrifice of the Mass and the sacraments of the Church. My heart is at pain, together with the Sacred Heart of Jesus and the Immaculate Heart of Mary, for those parents who must witness their own children grow to maturity without the benefits of true worship and instructions in the holy Christian faith.

Almighty God, the souls of those men, who are actually committed to atheistic communism, are also made in your image and likeness. They too have immortal souls. Forgive them and bring them to the light of faith in your Son made man. You have confided the peace of the world into the hands and heart of your blessed Mother who is our Mother too.

At Fatima she said, "In the end my Immaculate Heart shall triumph." But before that end comes, men must turn in faith, prayer, love and penance to the Sacred Heart of your Son, Jesus Christ. These two hearts, the Sacred Heart of Jesus and the Immaculate Heart of Mary, hold the secret, the source and means to freedom, love and peace for all men.

Your Immaculate Heart, O Mary, I know, can triumph, only by your bringing men to the Sacred Heart of your Son. In the love and mercy of the Sacred Heart, men will rest secure in the life of the blessed Trinity.

I wish to offer my prayers and penances of this day, in union with the holy sacrifice of the Mass around the world, for the conversion of Russia and all peoples of all nations, who in any way are deprived of truth and justice, freedom and peace in living their daily lives of work and recreation, worship and family living, for the glory of God and the salvation of souls. Amen.

Prayer for Peace

Lord Jesus Christ, who did say to your apostles: "Peace I leave unto you, my peace I give unto you, not as the world gives do I give unto you," consider not my sins but your merits, and grant to all your servants, that those whom the Father almighty has created and of whom he takes care, and whom you have redeemed with your precious blood and destined to eternal life may all love one another most cordially for your sake, may be of one heart, and may rejoice in your abiding peace.

Lord Jesus Christ, of whom the prophet sang: "All the kings of the earth shall do him homage, all the nations shall be submissive to his will," extend your rule to every human soul. Send forth the light of your faith upon all men, deliver them from the seductions and the bondage of passion, and turn their hearts to heavenly things. Grant likewise, of your goodness, that all nations and all races may be made one by holy Mother Church, your spouse, and that through the intercession of the blessed Virgin Mary, queen of peace, they may subject themselves to you in all humility. And from every tongue and people, may one same voice arise to sing your praise by day and by night, to bless you and extol you, O king of nations and sovereign Lord of all, O prince of peace, O deathless king of ages. Amen.

Prayer for Protection Of One's Home

Almighty God, keep our home and all who dwell in it safe from all harm of the evil spirits. Preserve us in mind, body and soul. Deliver our home from fire, storm and destruction of any kind. May our home be a sanctuary of love, a place of growth in the likeness of Jesus, a temple of the domestic Church.

Holy immaculate Mother of God and glorious St. Joseph, protector and patron of our homes, save and protect us now and at the hour of our death. Amen.